The Literature of Cinema

ADVISORY EDITOR: MARTIN S. DWORKIN
INSTITUTE OF PHILOSOPHY AND POLITICS OF EDUCATION
TEACHER'S COLLEGE, COLUMBIA UNIVERSITY

THE LITERATURE OF CINEMA presents
a comprehensive selection from the multitude
of writings about cinema, rediscovering materials on its origins, history, theoretical principles and techniques, aesthetics, economics,
and effects on societies and individuals. Included are works of inherent, lasting merit
and others of primarily historical significance.
These provide essential resources for serious
study and critical enjoyment of the "magic
shadows" that became one of the decisive cul-
tural forces of modern times.

Animated Photography
The ABC of the Cinematograph

Cecil M. Hepworth

ARNO PRESS & THE NEW YORK TIMES
New York • 1970

Reprint Edition 1970 by Arno Press Inc.
Reprinted from a copy in The Museum of Modern Art Library
Library of Congress Catalog Card Number: 73-124009
ISBN 0-405-01615-8
ISBN for complete set: 0-405-01600-X
Manufactured in the United States of America

243654

ANIMATED
PHOTOGRAPHY

THE A B C OF THE

CINEMATOGRAPH

A SIMPLE AND THOROUGH GUIDE TO
THE PROJECTION OF LIVING PHOTOGRAPHS, WITH
NOTES ON THE PRODUCTION OF
CINEMATOGRAPH NEGATIVES

BY
CECIL M. HEPWORTH

SECOND EDITION
REVISED AND BROUGHT UP TO DATE BY
HECTOR MACLEAN

[THE AMATEUR PHOTOGRAPHER'S LIBRARY, NO. 14.]

London
HAZELL, WATSON, & VINEY, LD.
1, CREED LANE, LUDGATE HILL, E.C.
1900

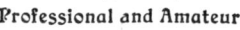

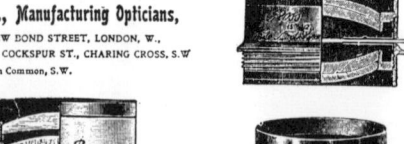
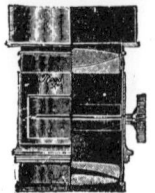

PREFACE TO SECOND EDITION.

IN bringing the present issue up to date, it is thought best not to tamper with Mr. Hepworth's lucid and interesting text, but confine attention to supplying such additions as circumstances call for, and allow, in the shape of a series of paragraphs, forming a concluding chapter.

In this particular attention has been given to the needs of *The Amateur Cinematographist*, who, until quite lately, has been much neglected. Recent experiences, however, indicate that, so far from cinematography being outside the sphere of the amateur, it is steadily gaining ground in his favour ; indeed, there is reason to think that, as the apparatus and materials become improved, not only will many amateurs take up the practice of Animated Photography, but they will, on account of their number, and of their enthusiasm, at times obtain results which the comparatively few professional operators do not enjoy the opportunities of achieving.

HECTOR MACLEAN,

CROYDON, *March* 1900.

CONTENTS.

CHAP		PAGE
	INTRODUCTORY	1
I.	CINEMATOGRAPH PICTURES	6
II.	THE OPTICAL SYSTEM	12
III.	THE MECHANICAL SYSTEM	18
IV.	INTERMITTENT MECHANISM	23
V.	CONTINUOUS MECHANISM	37
VI.	THE SHUTTER	52
VII.	ILLUMINANTS: THE LIMELIGHT	59
VIII.	THE ELECTRIC ARC LIGHT	65
IX.	COMBINATION OF LANTERN AND CIMEMATOGRAPH	73
X.	PRECAUTIONS AGAINST DANGER	79
XI.	HINTS AND CAUTIONS: CARE OF CINEFILMS, ETC.	83
XII.	CINEMATOGRAPHIC CAMERAS	89
XIII.	ON TAKING ANIMATED PHOTOGRAPHS	94
XIV.	DEVELOPING, PRINTING, ETC.	99
XV.	ALTERNATE PROJECTION WITH TWO LENSES	105
XVI.	NOTES ON CINEMATOGRAPHY IN 1900	109

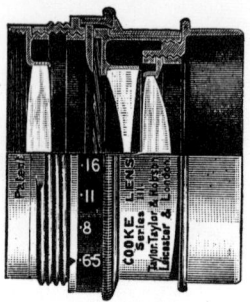

ANIMATED PHOTOGRAPHY.

INTRODUCTORY.

INTERESTING as is the history of the cinematograph,
and instructive as the contemplation of its development
from its early prototype—the zoetrope—I do not propose to
dilate upon this branch of the subject in the present instance.
The object of this little book is not in any sense historical;
its aim is merely to put in convenient form the salient
features of cinematography as at present understood.

With this end in view it will only be necessary, by way
of introduction, to briefly trace the development of the
machine from the crude toy in which it found its earliest
conception, or rather, to hint at a few of the successive
stages by which it arrived at its present degree of development. The zoetrope, in its simplest form, consisted of a
disc of card, upon which were painted, at regular intervals
around its periphery, a number of consecutive images of
one figure, representing it in various phases of one continuous movement, each image being slightly more pro-
gressed than its immediate predecessor.

Below each picture was a narrow slit cut through the
card, and the manner of using the toy was to hold it up
facing a mirror, and twirl it upon a pin passed through its
centre. The drawings were then viewed through the slits
from the back, as reflected in the looking-glass, and the
figures, although stationary as a whole, appeared to have
movement imparted to their limbs as the disc was twirled.
A quaint parody of natural movements in truth it was
that was enacted by the little figures; for the artist,

1

having little else to guide him, drew largely upon his own
fertile imagination for his ideas of the analysis of motion,
and the result, when synthesised in the instrument, was
often extremely grotesque.   Nevertheless, there was a
certain fascination about the jumping figures which induced
many to attempt to apply the device to the optical lantern.
It was soon found, however, that the very small amount of
light which the slits in the shutter-disc would transmit to
the screen was far too meagre, especially as these slits had
to be made considerably smaller than before, in order to
give the sharper definition demanded by the exigencies of
the magnification to which they were subjected.

But one of these experimenters adopted a different basis
for his experiments, and in his choreutoscope, as he called
their result, was embodied a principle without which none
of the cinematographs of the present day would be of
any use

In this little instrument, which, by the way, was small
enough for the slide-stage of an ordinary lantern, the
pictures were arranged on a flat strip, which an ingenious
escapement mechanism was made to pass through the
lantern in a series of jerks with a pause between each.
The pictures were supported on a travelling brass strip,
having a notch below each ; and an eccentric beneath,
as it turned, shifted it forward one step in a revolution.
Immediately in front of the pictures was a little shutter
which descended and cut off the light at each movement,
and immediately reopened again as soon as the picture had
come to rest.   Thus in this instrument of strange name was
the embryo of the modern cinematograph ; and although
the patronymic has not been inherited, the tendency to high-
flown nomenclature certainly has, and the names assumed
by the present-day machines would make even the inventor
of the choreutoscope tremble.

When instantaneous photography became an accomplished
fact, several workers turned their attention to the production
of successive photographs representing the movements of
various objects in different phases.   Most of the photographs
were taken for the purpose of scientific investigation,
wherein these analyses of movements were, as may be supposed, very valuable.   One of the most notable productions

of its kind was the famous "Trotting Horse," taken by Muybridge, of California, in which, by the employment of a large number of separate photographic cameras arranged side by side, successive photographs of a horse in different phases of movement were made as the beast passed along the course in front of the cameras, and automatically released the shutter of each as he passed. Although those series photographs were taken at far too long intervals of time between each to be of practical value for after synthesis and viewing as one animated picture, Mr. Muybridge did produce series photographs with this object, and even succeeded in projecting them for the illustration of his lectures on the subject.

As may be supposed, the battery of separate cameras, each with a separate shutter capable of being released at intervals, was soon discarded in favour of the far more convenient arrangement by which one camera was made to impress successive images on a rapidly moving plate or series of plates passed behind the lens, the rotary shutter transmitting a flash of light to each as it came into position. Such a camera was that invented by Anschutz, whereby the series photographs were taken far more perfectly and at much shorter intervals. The synthesis of these series photographs by means of the zoetrope, or "wheel of life," followed as a matter of course, and that little instrument blossomed out again into public favour to a certain extent when fed with photo-lithographs from the camera of Anschutz. By means of a glorified zoetrope, which he called the Living Wonder, Anschutz succeeded in electrifying the whole world for a few days with the marvellously life-like reproductions of natural movements. In this instrument the photographic transparencies on glass were arranged around the periphery of a large wheel revolving behind a lens through which the pictures were viewed. There was no shutter, but its place was taken by a most ingenious arrangement, by whose aid a brilliant electric spark from an induction machine was made to illuminate each little picture precisely as it came into position.

More than one experimenter attempted to adapt this at that time marvellous machine to lantern projection, but the electric spark upon a sufficiently brilliant scale was impracticable—indeed, impossible—and no other contrivance could take its place, so the result was nothing but failure.

The next remarkable achievement was the Edison kinetoscope, which was simply a modification of the Living Wonder, suggested by the late improvement in photography, by which really satisfactory photographs upon a flexible support could be produced by the aid of transparent celluloid. Edison used a rotating shutter, with a very narrow slit in it, in place of the electric spark, and as his pictures were very much smaller he found adequate illumination in an incandescent electric lamp placed immediately under the film picture. By the use of celluloid, and by confining himself to very small pictures, he was able to produce an almost incredible number in a given space of time, and to continue to produce them at this rate until there were enough to record a complete little episode. Thus in the kinetoscope there were forty feet of film accommodating no less than six hundred little photographs, arranged one above the other, and measuring one inch broad by about five-eighths high.

In the meantime other experimenters were at work upon the same idea, notably an Englishman, Mr. Birt Acres, who was successful in making series photographs some years ago. He actually exhibited an early form of cinematograph of his own design, before the Photographic Society of Great Britain, as early as January 1895.

With these wonderfully perfect series photographs of Edison's at their command, it is no wonder that before very long other inventors succeeded in producing a machine by which they could be projected upon a lantern screen. It was not, however, until they turned their attention to the revival of the almost forgotten intermittent motion as used in Beale's choreutoscope, that any practical result was possible. Then it became merely a matter of the mechanical contrivance by which the desired result should be obtained, and at that point the various experimenters diverged and struck out, each a line of his own ; and it is upon that point that the last word has at the present time not yet been spoken.

It was soon found that Edison's series photographs—perfect as they were in many ways—could be much improved upon for projection work. Their chief sin was a density that no light could satisfactorily pierce; and directly the later workers learned to take the pictures for themselves, they were relegated to disuse. They were taken with a rapidity which is found unnecessary, and the forty exposures per second has now been reduced to nearer twenty, and often less, in a similar time.

Having thus scantily paved the way for a consideration of the projection machine of the present day, it is proposed to call in review, not the instruments themselves—for a dealer's catalogue will do that—but the various mechanical principles which they represent. It was feared that completeness could hardly be hoped for in the present state of the art, when fresh machines embodying fresh principles are of almost every-day occurrence, and so it was decided to confine the descriptions to those instruments that have come under the author's personal knowledge, and many of which he has himself used.

CHAPTER I.

CINEMATOGRAPH PICTURES.

WHEN the Edison kinetoscope was introduced, a certain set of dimensions for the little pictures was arbitrarily selected and closely adhered to, in order that the subjects might be interchangeable in the instruments. And the vast majority of the inventors who turned their attention to the projection on a lantern screen of these living photographs which had attracted so much notice, naturally selected for their earlier experiments the series photographs, as they might be called, which were ready to their hands. To make and use a camera for actually taking these series photographs was a task that very few attempted : it was so much easier to procure the excellent pictures that had already been produced for use in the kinetoscope, and to then construct a suitable instrument for their projection upon the screen.

And so it came about that the arbitrary measurements which had been selected by Edison were perpetuated in the earlier cinematographs. It was soon seen, however, that the Edison pictures, though wonderfully perfect for the purpose for which they were originally intended, were in very many respects unsuitable for projection. In the first place they were exceedingly dense. Photographic density within reasonable limits was no detriment in a kinetoscope, for the brilliant little incandescent lamp, by whose light the picture was viewed, was quite sufficient to illuminate a fairly thick transparency ; but the case was entirely different when it came to projecting these little transparencies upon the lantern screen. For in a cinematograph there are many things which militate against brilliancy of a projected picture; and even now, when many of the earlier difficulties have been successfully overcome, with the most perfected instruments there is never so much light that a little more would not be a decided advantage. The fact that the Edison pictures were far too dense to be satisfactorily projected was recognised in the very early days of cinematography, and it was not long before this part of the question began to receive the attention that it deserved; but by that time several projection machines had been evolved from the workshops of the earlier experimenters, and in these the Edison standard had been adopted. Naturally enough, therefore, when these earlier experimenters began to make their own films, they adhered to the style to which they had become accustomed. Thus the old Edison kinetoscope standard is the standard of the present day.

But in the course of the endeavours which were constantly being made to overcome the inherent faults of cinematography—flickering of the light, and, more especially in the early days, unsteadiness of the picture upon the screen—the idea naturally suggested itself that if it were not necessary to magnify the pictures to such an extreme extent in order to procure a fair-sized image, the unsteadiness would be very considerably reduced. One or two inventors therefore broke away from the beaten track of Edison standardism, and commenced to make the series pictures on a scale which would bring them more on a level with an ordinary lantern slide. Undoubtedly the finest results that have yet been obtained have been arrived at by this means, but there are many disadvantages which must be placed to its account.

To make these series photographs three inches across instead of one inch, as hitherto, means, of course, each picture being nine times the size of those previously used, and that the original outlay for sensitive film would be nine times as much as would suffice under the older conditions. That alone is a very heavy consideration, for even as matters stand under the usual conditions it costs about £1 to buy sufficient film for one negative of average size, and then a similar outlay for the positive; and when this expense is added to all the others that are incidental, and due allowance is made for unavoidable waste, the idea of multiplying the sum by nine suggests the thought that cinematography is out of the question for any but million-aires. Then again, eighty feet of wet and light-sensitive film—about the average length at the present time—is, as it is, somewhat unwieldy to handle in the darkroom. The idea of handling two hundred and forty feet of such material suggests visions of profanity that is abhorrent to the mind of the religiously disposed. As a further evidence against the use of large pictures, it may be mentioned that the mechanical difficulties of moving such a mass of material with the necessary intermittent motion through the projection machine are very much greater than where the smaller strip is concerned.

And so, in spite of the undeniable advantages of the system, the use of large pictures has not come into general favour, and the Edison dimensions may be taken as a standard to which there are no more than the usual number of dissentients. According to this system, the size of each little picture of a series is one inch broad by five-eighths of an inch high. They are printed by photography upon a strip of sensitised celluloid film, and their arrangement is such that they are one on the top of the other—not side by side—and there is no appreciable space between one little picture and the next.

To pass a strip of sensitive celluloid behind a lens, and by means of a rotary shutter to make a number of photo-graphic exposures upon it at regular intervals, would not appear to present much difficulty; but to re-pass that strip in a similar manner through a lantern, and to un-cover it exactly as each little image takes up its position behind the lens so that the pictures are thrown upon the screen in a series of flashes, presents much greater difficul-ties. It is conceivable that no skill or accuracy in the construction of the mechanism would infallibly ensure the equal feeding of the film through the instrument so exactly that each little picture should always be precisely behind the lens at the moment that the shutter opened. The slight variations in the sizes of rollers which are bound to follow upon variations in temperature would be quite sufficient to derange the mechanism and ultimately throw the pictures completely out of place, even if the film itself did not constantly vary in length.

This difficulty as to the registration of the pictures—the exact superposition of one picture precisely over the place immediately before occupied by its predecessor—is overcome by notching the film a certain number of times for each picture, and providing upon the rollers by which it is drawn forward corresponding pegs to engage with the notches.

Here again a standard has been established that is more or less generally adhered to. In the kinetoscope the picture strips were one and three-eighths inches broad, and, the one-inch picture being printed in the middle, there was an unoccupied space of three-sixteenths of an inch on either side. In this space there were a number of cushion-shaped perforations through the film, and these were about a square sixteenth of an inch in size, so that there was a strip of unperforated film an eighth of an inch broad outside the perforations.

With one notable exception all the inventors of the instruments for the projection of the living photographs who adhered to the Edison standard for the size of the pictures also copied the system of perforation : thus we find that nearly all the commercial films of the present day are perforated with a row of holes down either side ; these holes vary a little in size, though they are approximately that which has been quoted ; they vary in shape somewhat also, some being square, some oblong, and some cushion-shaped. None of these slight variations are sufficient to make the film pictures uninterchangeable on most of the machines at present in use. The pictures are always approximately the same height, and there are invariably four holes on either side of the film to each picture.

I have said that the pictures on films supplied by different makers vary slightly in height, and it follows, therefore, that there must be also a slight difference in the distance apart of the perforations, seeing that there are always four holes to a picture. Thus, if you hold up to the light, one over the other, two films by different makers, you will rarely find that the rows of holes will exactly correspond for more

than a short distance. Sometimes the difference is noticeable
in a couple of inches ; in others, the holes may seem to
correspond for a foot or more.

The films are drawn forward in the apparatus by means
of a cylinder, or cylinders, having a row of little pegs on
the surface near either extremity which engage with these
perforations. So long as only a dozen or so of these pegs
engage with the film at one time, the slight variations in
the spaces between the holes will not give much trouble.
It is when the cylinder is of large diameter and the film
passes a considerable distance around it, or when there are

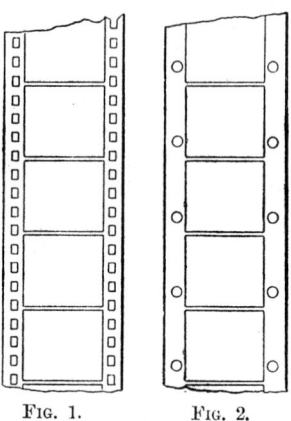

Fɪɢ. 1.   Fɪɢ. 2.

two toothed cylinders and the film is stretched tightly
between them, that the trouble arises from this want of
uniformity. Under these circumstances a film that does
not fit rapidly gets torn, and a film that is much torn is
useless.

A single variant from the Edison standard of perforation
has been mentioned as being specially notable. This was
one of the very first instruments to be introduced, but, unlike
most of its near contemporaries, is still one of the very
best machines that there is. Although the same dimensions
of picture and the same size of film are used in this machine,
the system of perforation is different. The plan adopted is

to pierce one round hole on either side of each picture, and as this hole is always in exactly the same position with reference to the picture, one of the adjustments necessary in machines on the Edison system is satisfactorily dispensed with.

The illustrations on the opposite page represent a few inches of picture film according to these two principal systems. That on the right (fig. 2) shows the manner of perforation of a "one-hole" film, and that on the left (fig. 1) the system used in all other machines except, of course, those designed for pictures of larger size. This last is called the Edison "four-hole" system ; and although, as has been already pointed out, there are considerable variations from the original model, they are not of sufficient magnitude to render the varying films unsuitable for most of the Edison standard machines at present on the market.

CHAPTER II.

THE OPTICAL SYSTEM.

TO him who contemplates the manipulation of a cinematograph, either for pleasure or profit or any other
reason, a thorough knowledge of the principles on which
the living photographs are based, and of the various
mechanical devices by which the results are sought to be
brought about, is of the utmost value. It will, first of all,
be no inconsiderable help to him in the choice of an instrument, and that is a most important point; for there is a
wonderful array of instruments to choose from, and they
vary through all degrees of efficiency from the most
abominable of " St. Vituscopes "—as it has been suggested
that all cinematographs should be generally called—to the
nearest approach to perfection that has at present been
obtained. And secondly, such a knowledge will be of the
greatest service to him, not only in enabling him to so
manipulate the apparatus that it is exhibited to the highest
of its efficiency, but it will also give him the power of
locating faults whenever they occur—as they are bound
to do occasionally—and very possibly of remedying the
derangement with as little delay as possible.

A knowledge, too, of the optical principle and the mechanical arrangements of the cinematograph will give the operator
confidence in his instrument; and confidence, as every
public entertainer knows full well, is one of the first attributes
of success. It is difficult to think of any likely plight for
the lanternist more miserable than to be operating before
a large audience an instrument with whose characteristics
and peculiarities he is quite unfamiliar. He is filled with
misgiving regarding its behaviour: he does not trust his

apparatus, and he is all the time miserably conscious that should anything go wrong, as he feels vaguely may happen at any moment, he is utterly powerless to put it right.

No apology, therefore, is, I think, needed for the space which it is proposed to devote to a full consideration of, first, the general principles of cinematographic projection, and, second, the various mechanical devices that have from time to time been brought forward by which this principle is more or less perfectly carried out.

In order the more readily to comprehend the optical arrangements by which the moving photographs are projected upon the lantern screen, let us glance for a moment at a diagram of an ordinary optical lantern system. For it must be remembered that the lantern portion of a cinematograph differs only in one small particular from the

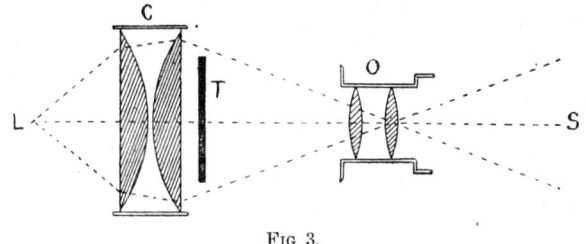

Fig 3.

arrangements of the older instrument which is so familiar to all of us as the optical or magic lantern.

The diagram which I have re-drawn for this page must be more than familiar to the majority of my readers, for it has appeared over and over again in various periodicals and in all the text-books on the lantern ; but it is included here for the sake of completeness, and in order to refresh the memories of such as may be not sufficiently familiar with the interior economy of an ordinary optical lantern that they can altogether dispense with a short description before proceeding to a consideration of the cinematograph.

In the diagram before you (fig. 3) L represents the source of light whose chief characteristics should always be the maximum of brilliancy with the minimum of size. In other words, the light should be the most brilliant that it

is possible to obtain, but its luminous area must be small.
The nearer it approaches the beau ideal of an Euclidean
point the better will be the resultant picture in all respects
  From the source of light the rays spread out in all
directions within the limits of its illuminating angle, following, of course, the "law of inverse squares," by which
its intensity diminishes as the *square* of the distance. c is
the condenser usually formed of two plano-convex lenses
placed with their convex sides almost in contact with one
another.   Their diameter should be just a little larger than
the longest diagonal, or diameter of the transparency,
T, whose image is to be projected upon the screen. o is
the projecting lens, or objective placed at such a distance
from the slide that the image of the latter is correctly
focussed upon the distant screen in front of it : that is to
say, that the slide is placed at one of its conjugate foci
while the screen is at the other.   The objective itself
occupies the position of one of the conjugate foci of the
condenser, so that all the rays of light, as rendered conver-
gent by the latter, are able to pass through it.   As the
source of light, L, must naturally be placed at the other
conjugate focus of the condenser, it follows that its position
behind the lens not only depends upon the focal length of
the condenser, but also upon that of the objective ; also,
with every variation of the distance of the screen in front
of the projecting lens, the distance of the slide behind it
must be correspondingly varied, for they are placed at the
respective conjugate foci of the lens.   But the slide is not
moved, because its proper position is close up to the condenser ; therefore the front lens must be altered in distance
from the condenser and slide in order to obtain variations
in focus.   And that means that the position of the light
must also be correspondingly altered in order to maintain
the balance that is necessary to perfect results.
  I have said that the slide should be placed close up to
the condenser.   The usual size for a lantern condenser is
four inches in diameter, because that is a little larger than
the diagonal measurement for the largest lantern-slide opening that is ever used at the present time.   If the transparency, T, were not close up to the condenser, but some
little distance away from it, it would intersect the cone

of light rays at a point where they would be insufficiently spread out to embrace the whole of the slide opening; the corners of the pictures would therefore be cut off by shadow. But if the condenser were larger, it would then be right to place the slide at some distance from it, so that the cone of rays might be intersected at a point where they were sufficiently *condensed* to pass through the opening; otherwise the light upon the screen would be unduly attenuated, on account of the fact that only a portion of it would be able to find its way through the slide.

In practice the advantages of using a larger condenser are not apparent, except in those cases where it is necessary to use so powerful a source of light that it is impracticable to place it at the usual distance from the glass, for fear of damage from the intense heat: for where the source of light must on this account be removed to a greater distance from the condenser, that lens must necessarily be of longer focus; and as the source of light is farther away, and the condenser still of the same diameter, the proportion of light rays which it would collect would be very much smaller, because the intensity of the light diminishes as the square of the distance from its source. Hence we are no better off than with a less powerful light at a smaller distance. In this case it is advisable to use a condenser of larger diameter, so as to embrace a larger angle with reference to the position of the light, and to place it at such a distance behind the slide that the latter cuts the cone of rays at the most advantageous point.

It might therefore be supposed that where we have a very small-sized slide to deal with, it would only be necessary to reduce the size of every other part of the apparatus in due proportion. And so it would, were it possible to do so. But it is not possible to reduce the size of the source of light without impairing its brilliancy, and then only to a limited extent. As it is, our only available light sources are too large in luminous area to be really satisfactory, and for cinematographs they are larger than for ordinary lantern work, for so much more illumination is demanded of them.

Hence the almost universal practice is to employ a light source and condensing lens of the usual lantern

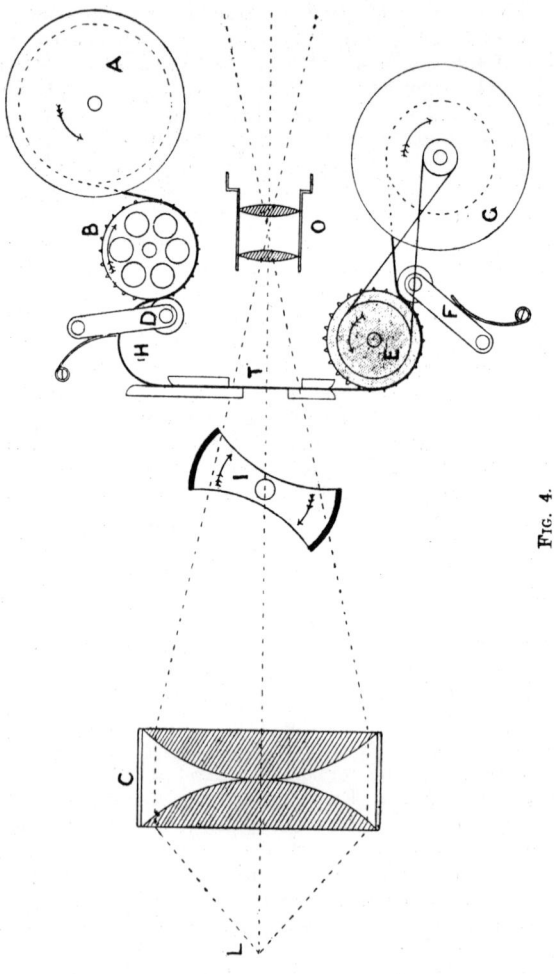

FIG. 4.

pattern in a cinematograph, and to push the tiny picture that has to be projected so far along the cone of rays that the light can pass almost entirely through it, and with as little loss around the edges as may be. A front lens of proportionately short focus must of course be used in connection with this small transparency, or the image upon the screen would be very small indeed.

So much, then, for the slight difference between the optical system of an ordinary lantern and that of a cinematograph. Now let us consider the latter a little more fully.

In the diagram upon the opposite page (fig. 4) I have endeavoured to plan out in simple form the essential portions of a complete cinematograph in such a manner that it may be easily comprehended. All details have been omitted, and only those portions included as are absolutely necessary to the elucidation of the principle upon which all living photographic apparatus are constructed.

First as to the optical arragements. As in the preceding diagram, L is the source of light, and c the condenser, whose duty it is to collect the divergent rays from the lamp and squeeze them together, as it were, and so cause them to converge upon the projecting lens, o. The transparency, T, instead of being close up to the condenser, where it would take in but a very small proportion of the available light, on account of its comparatively small size, has been moved much farther forward, and in this position it embraces nearly the whole bundle of rays. That is all. The rest of the arrangement is simply a mechanical device for changing the little pictures with the necessary rapidity.

2

CHAPTER III.

THE MECHANICAL SYSTEM.

THERE are two great classes into which all the practical cinematographs of the present day may be roughly separated. In the one class are all those instruments in which the necessary intermittent motion of the film is applied to it through the medium of intermittently moving mechanism; in the other, the motion of the mechanical contrivance is continuous or, at all events, reciprocal, and its action upon one portion of the film is such that intermittent motion is applied to it.

It is in the former class that we must look to find the majority of the recognised instruments, and we may as well, therefore, deal with this, the larger class, first. But it must not be supposed that the greater merit necessarily rests with the instruments that are to be found therein. As a matter of fact, machines that have met with very great favour are to be found under either category.

As a preliminary to the following consideration of some of the various methods that have from time to time been devised to meet the requirements of cinematography, let me briefly call to mind the circumstances under which the living photographs are produced, and review the difficulties that have to be met and overcome.

We have, then, a strip of celluloid, one and three-eighths inches wide, and, say, seventy-five feet in length. It is coated with a film of gelatine—the vehicle which carries the photographic impression. The photograph takes the form of a series of little pictures, an inch broad and five-eighths high, printed one just over the other, and quite close together. There are about twelve hundred of these little pictures, and they are all very similar to one another, yet each one is slightly different from all the rest—that is to say, they each represent the same scene, but each presents a slightly different phase. They are the result of a photographic analysis of a series of movements, as it were. Properly synthesised, they will reproduce those movements exactly as they were originally.

To synthesise these little pictures so as to reproduce these movements as they originally appeared, it is necessary to view them in as rapid succession as that in which they were produced—say, fifteen in a second. The change from one picture to the next must be so quickly accomplished that it is indiscernible to the eye, and each picture must drop absolutely into the same place as that but an instant before occupied by its predecessor. Moreover, the change from one picture to the next—seeing that it cannot be accomplished instantaneously—must be covered by a period of darkness, otherwise, by the phenomenon known as " persistence of vision," the impression received by the retina while the picture is moving will remain over into the period of rest, and give a blurred appearance to the picture.

If the reader will refer back again to the diagram of the cinematograph system on page 16, it will be seen that, robbed of all its unessential accessories, the cinematograph is really a comparatively simple instrument after all. It consists merely of a mechanical movement, whose object it is to pass the photographic film forward past the lens system intermittently, moving it exactly one picture's breadth at each jerk; and a shutter, by which the light is cut off during those periods of movement, but is allowed free passage all the while the picture is still.

To begin at the beginning, A is the spool on which the picture film is wound. In many of the most modern machines this spool is done away with, its place being taken by a peg, which forms an axle on which is placed the roll of film. Where the film is drawn down in jerks—as it always is, unless there be a special contrivance to feed it continuously—this method has the advantage of presenting as little inertia as possible to the intermittent tugs. A spool of metal or other material must necessarily have inertia, which has to be continually overcome, and thus a considerable strain is put upon the film ; while if the spool run very freely, it is liable to spin faster than the film is required, and thus the danger of entanglement is introduced. On the other hand, where the film is of great length, or where there are a number of films joined together, it is not practicable to put so large a coil unsupported upon a peg, and the spool becomes a necessity.

For this reason, there is great preference, in my opinion, for machines in which there is a continuous feed of film, and the intermittent motion only communicated to a few inches of the film instead of constantly tugging at the whole supply. In the imaginary machine now under consideration I have provided for this by means of the drum, B.

This drum, or barrel, is technically called a "sprocket wheel." It is a cylinder, generally of brass, and hollow or solid according to taste, bearing on its surface, near either end, a row of pegs, or sprockets, which engage with the perforation of the film, and thus ensures the exact amount of "feed" required. As there are four perforations on either side of each picture—it is called the "four-hole" system—it follows that the number of teeth on either side of any sprocket wheel must be some multiple of four in order that at each revolution it may draw forward or feed the pictures integrally. Thus, a sprocket wheel having twenty-four teeth at either end will feed forward no more or less than six pictures for each completed revolution. It would be technically called a "six-picture wheel."

In the diagram now under consideration, there are two sprocket wheels, and each are of "six-picture" capacity. It follows that if both revolve at precisely the same rate, a piece of film may be passed first around one and then on to the other ; and whatever capacity the loop of film between them may originally have, it will always remain constant until the end. But to proceed.

The film passes about half way round the sprocket wheel, B, with which it is held in contact by the pressure roller, having grooves cut in it to make room for the teeth of the cylinder. Thence it passes in an unrestricted loop to the projection point, where it is held sufficiently tightly between two pressure plates, which serve to keep it flat and at the correct focal distance from the objective, o. After that, it is taken up by another sprocket wheel, similar to the first except in one respect, presently to be explained, and thence it goes to a receiving spool, G.

And now for the difference between those two sprocket wheels. The upper one, B, is merely to feed the film forward continuously, so as to relieve the spool of the intermittent tugging. It therefore turns *continuously*. The other cylinder has a more important work to perform. To its share falls the duty of imparting the necessary intermittent motion to the film ; therefore it is so connected with the mechanism that it turns in a series of jerks—six to each complete revolution—so that exactly one picture, no more and no less, is pulled through at each jerk. The two sprocket wheels revolve at exactly the same rate, in spite of the difference in their manner of revolving. That is to say, each completes a revolution at the same instant, and, of course in each case, six pictures are passed through the instrument for each revolution. Thus the loop, H, between the picture point and the feeding sprocket, always remains of constant capacity : it simply rises and falls as one sprocket wheel gains a little on the other for a moment and then halts until the balance is restored.

In the diagram the sprocket, E, is at rest, and the picture is therefore stationary at the little window, T. The sprocket, B, is still moving, of course, but it is merely feeding forward enough film—augmenting the loop, H,— to be ready for the next jerk—the next change of picture. There is no other obstruction to the light, which therefore follows the direction of the dotted lines, and reproduces the little picture which happens to be at the window, T, immensely enlarged upon the screen.

It has been said that at the instant that this little picture is moved forward and its place taken by the next one of the series, the light must be shut off so that the movement is not apparent on the screen. This is accomplished by the shutter, I, which, being double acting, as it were, makes but half a revolution to each picture. The form of this shutter is not very clear from the drawing. It really consists of a flat strip of metal, say, nine inches long by one inch broad. This is divided into three equal lengths, and the end pieces bent up at right angles to the middle part, so as to form a letter U (*see* fig. 16, " Cylindrical shutter"). The middle of the centre portion is attached to a pivot, and the U is placed horizontally. It is the end of this pivot which can be seen in the diagram, and the turned-up edges are shown as thick black lines. In various makes of instruments the shutter takes various forms, but it is generally either of this pattern or of the shape of a fan or segment of a disc.

In the present case the shutter revolves three times for every turn of the sprocket wheels. At every half revolution the light is cut off, and the little picture changed from one to the next.

This outline description is applicable in most particulars to all the cinematographs that belong to this first great class—those which have a sprocket wheel that moves inter- mittently and thus imparts the necessary intermittent motion to the film. It is in the manner by which this intermittent motion is applied to the sprocket wheel that the various machines of this class differ from one another, and the various mechanical movements—or at all events, a few that are fairly representative—will be dealt with in the next chapter. Then there will still remain that class of instruments in which the intermittent motion is derived by the film direct from continuously or reciprocally moving mechanism without the intervention of any jerkily actuated contrivances whatever. This class of instruments will receive due attention in a later chapter.

CHAPTER IV.

INTERMITTENT MECHANISM

IT has been said that a very large proportion of the living photograph machines that have up to the present been invented may be classed together under one category—instruments in which the necessary jerky motion of the film is accomplished by drawing it forward through the medium of an intermittently rotating sprocket wheel. And I have pointed out that in the large number of machines that depend upon this principle, there are several different methods by which this intermittent movement is imparted to the sprocket wheel. It is upon these different methods of changing the continuous motion of the handle into the intermittent movement of the toothed cylinder that the claims to letters patent rest—more or less insecurely. It is obvious that it would not be possible to secure a valid patent upon the general principle of the cinematograph, though, of course, our delightfully obliging Patent Office would willingly grant you full " protection "—if you paid for it—without having the least intention of helping you in any way if some one else jumped your claim. They would just as gladly grant you letters patent for a cinematograph as they would for the steam engine or the tea kettle or anything else you might like to "humbly pray" for, provided you paid the necessary fees in advance. But the patent would not be worth the paper it was printed upon.

It is hoped that these simple descriptions of some of the better known contrivances by which the intermittent motion is applied to the sprocket wheel may not only prove instructive to those interested in cinematography, but may also be a useful guide to possible buyers in enabling them to make intelligent choice between the thousand and one instruments with which they are confronted, all of which claim to be perfection and to have "complete absence of that flickering and unsteadiness that are so noticeable in other machines."

The "Maltese Cross" Movement.

This is one of the simplest movements that has ever been devised for this purpose, though not on that account necessarily the best; indeed, it is very far from being the

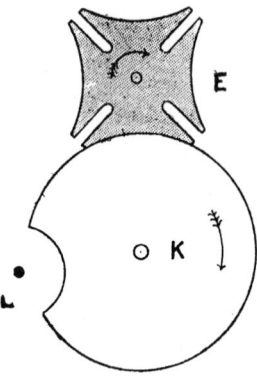

Fig. 5.

best, unless the machine is remarkably well made. In all these things nearly everything depends upon the workmanship; but the remark is perhaps more true of some than of others, and this certainly belongs to the former class.

The sketch (fig. 5) represents, in very diagrammatic fashion, the two principal wheels out of a cinematograph. As in all the other similar diagrams in this book, the wheel which moves intermittently is shaded, while that which has continuous motion is left blank. The upper, or shaded, wheel is in this case connected directly with the sprocket wheel, which is of the size to accommodate four pictures. The lower wheel is geared to the handle by which the instrument is operated, and is designed to turn at the rate of about fifteen revolutions per second—about the average speed at which living photographs are exhibited : for every complete revolution of this wheel draws one picture through the instrument, because it gives to the " maltese cross " wheel, and therefore to the sprocket wheel, a quarter turn every time.

The details of the movement will, I think, be fairly apparent from the drawing. When the mechanism is in the phase shown in the diagram, the "maltese cross " or " star " wheel is at rest ; and not only that, but it is tightly locked, so that no influence of inertia or gravity or anything else is able to move it. This locking of the sprocket wheel during its stationary periods is one of the most important points of a cinematograph with intermittently moving mechanism ; for if the cylinder simply came to rest of its own accord, so to speak, in the intervals between its periods of activity, with no special device for locking it fast in position, its inertia, or the weight of the film hanging from it, would be certain to drag it forward to a certain extent, and the extra movement would always be an uncertain quantity, and tend to very great unsteadiness of the projected picture.

In all these " star-wheel " movements the locking device is extremely simple, but it is liable to derangement after the instrument has been in use for a short time ; for a little wear—to which it is particularly liable—means a considerable amount of shake. As will be immediately apparent, the locking of the star wheel is secured by the smooth rim of the wheel, κ, pressing with sufficient tightness against the properly curved edge of the maltese cross. At one point on the periphery of the circular wheel there is a piece bitten out, as it were, of just sufficient size to release the edge of the maltese cross for a moment and allow it to make a quarter turn. This is accomplished by the peg, L, engaging in the radial slot between the arms of the cross. It slips into the slot which is proximate to it at the moment that the bitten out portion comes half under the cross and releases it from the grasp of the wheel, κ. The maltese cross wheel can only make one quarter turn at each complete revolution of the smooth wheel, and can only make it at the proper speed, for it is as tightly held in its period of motion by the little peg, L, as, in its time of rest, it is locked by the rim of the smooth wheel.

Of course due provision is made in the instrument for the lens to be covered by a shutter during the period of motion of the sprocket wheel.

It will be seen that this method of changing the continuous motion of the wheel, K, into the intermittent motion required in the sprocket wheel is one that has the advantage of extreme simplicity. But as I have said, the wear between the two edges that are in contact is considerable, as may be easily understood when it is remembered at what tremendous speed the wheel, K, revolves. When the two surfaces become, by wear, only slightly separated, a large amount of shake is introduced, with the inevitable result of causing unsteadiness of the picture on the screen.

Moreover, the sudden entrance of the peg into the radial slot, and, again, the equally sudden coming together of the edges of the two wheels when the one is brought to rest after one of its periods of movement, cause a loud tapping noise, which, occurring so many times in a second, develops into a sound that can only be described as very loud. I have heard machines built upon this principle emit a noise that one may modestly liken to a burglar alarm—resisting the obvious temptation to adopt a Hotchkiss gun as a simile.

But both of these objections may be to a very great extent overcome by good workmanship. If both wheels be made of suitable steel, the wear may be so far reduced that the efficient life of the instrument will be prolonged to a quite sufficient extent; while if the whole movement be made upon a comparatively small scale, and the curves really accurately worked out, the noise may be so far reduced that the machine may bear favourable comparison with many others in this respect also.

The " Double Star Wheel " Movement.

This is an amplification of the same principle—the Genever clutch—although, I believe, it is of earlier origin. Imagine the maltese cross movement, which has just been described, to be duplicated—that ·is to say, two maltese crosses, one on either side of the central smooth wheel ; the result of turning that central wheel will then be, of course, to impart intermittent motion to each of the star wheels alternately. Supposing each to be connected with a " four-picture " sprocket wheel, a piece of film might be stretched between the two, and the loop would be alternately loosened and tightened and at the same time passed forward a step at each turn of the central wheel. But if there were two pieces bitten out of the central wheel instead of one, and a peg in each, there would be two impulses imparted to each sprocket at every revolution ; and if the pegs were opposite to one another, the impulses would occur simultaneously in the two star wheels. Then the film stretched across the two sprockets would always be stretched with equal tension, and would be passed forward, one picture's breadth at a time, at every half revolution of the central wheel.

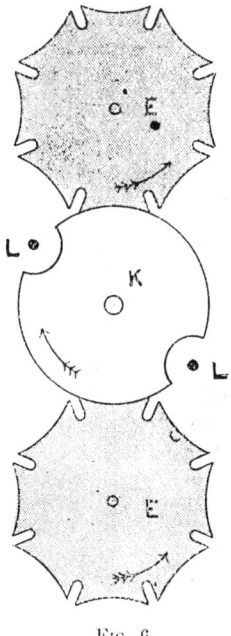

Fig. 6.

In most of the machines con-structed upon this principle the maltese cross is doubled in capacity, and therefore loses its characteristic appearance; and it is, of course, used in connection with an " eight-picture " sprocket wheel.

The arrangement is shown in simple diagrammatic form in fig. 6, where E and E are the upper and nether star wheels respectively, to which are attached the feeding and receiving sprocket wheels. K is the central smooth wheel which firmly locks both star wheels in their periods of rest, and L L are the actuating pegs by which they are moved round one-eighth of a turn, when the cut away portions come round and free them from restraint.

Naturally the objections which were urged against the single star wheel device last mentioned are doubled in the arrangement under present consideration, and, equally naturally, both objections may to a very great extent be overcome by good workmanship and careful attention to the causes of the trouble.

There is another objection to this duplex arrangement in which the film passes over two sprocket wheels moving simultaneously, which is, perhaps, less easily overcome ; and that rests upon the fact, on which stress has already been laid (*see* p. 9), that the distance between the perforations in films of different make is liable to considerable variation. If a film of exact Edison gauge fit over the two sprocket wheels in such a manner that it is stretched between them, neither too tightly nor too loosely, it is obvious that over the same pair of wheels, similarly adjusted, a film of longer or shorter perforation would either hang loosely, so as to give a wobbly picture, or it would be so tightly stretched as to be in danger of being torn to shreds. In the actual machines built upon this principle, I believe it is customary to so adjust the mechanism that all films will hang more or less loosely between the wheels, and are held steady by two pressure plates, as in the machine sketched on page 16. By that arrangement, of course, the two sprocket wheels are no better than one—in spite of the proverb ; indeed, they are rather worse, because of the objections already cited. It were far better to employ one sprocket moving intermittently and one running continuously to feed it with film, for by that means the detrimental intermittent tugging on the spool is entirely avoided.

There are other modifications of the " star-wheel " movement besides the two already described, some having " five pictures " and some six per revolution, and so on ; but enough has been said to indicate the principle.

The " Pawl and Ratchet " Movement.

It might appear at first sight that the simplest method of transforming continuous rotary motion into the intermittent movement required in cinematographs would be by

means of a pawl actuated by a crank operating on a
ratchet wheel. The method is certainly simple, and, if the
movement had to be made fifteen times per minute instead
of per second, would probably leave nothing to be desired.
But as it does not of itself provide any means of locking
the ratchet wheel between the thrusts of the pawl, it will
be seen that, as these thrusts occur so frequently and so

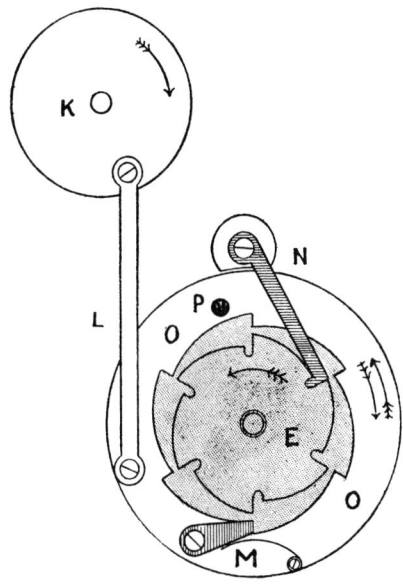

Fig. 7.

swiftly, the ratchet wheel would be carried forward after
each by its own momentum, and the steadiness of the picture
would become a very uncertain quantity.

With pawl and ratchet movements, therefore, it is necessary to combine an independent locking device for holding
the sprocket wheel stationary between the impulses.

All necessary requirements are admirably met in one
excellent machine, which is made upon this principle, and
whose movement is roughly outlined in the sketch above

(fig. 7). In the sketch those portions are, as usual, shaded which have intermittent motion, while those whose motion is continuous or reciprocal are left white.

At the upper part of the drawing the wheel, K, turns continuously at a speed of fifteen revolutions per second or thereabouts, for at every turn one little picture is exhibited and changed. This wheel acts the part of a crank or eccentric, and imparts reciprocating motion to the wheel, O O, by the instrumentality of the rod, L. The wheel, E, is a double ratchet wheel, free to revolve above the disk, O O, and is in direct communication with a " six-picture " sprocket wheel behind. It is made of ebonite, and is all in one piece. Leaving the upper pawl, N, out of the question for the present, it will be seen that every to-and-fro movement of the disk, as it is pushed and pulled by the rod, K, will cause the pawl, M, to engage in a fresh tooth of the ratchet wheel, and so force it round one-sixth of a revolution, provided it is prevented from turning in the opposite direction and thus setting up a to-and-fro movement like that of the plate on which it rests.

The pressure of the film-holding pads on the sprocket wheel is sufficient to prevent this return action of the ratchet; and so, if momentum could be ignored, the movement as so far described would be complete. But at the high rate of speed at which these things must work, it is necessary to provide a checking device, so that the mechanism shall not be carried forward farther than the required extent. In the instrument under consideration this necessity is provided for by means of a second ratchet wheel, with teeth facing in the reverse direction, and another pawl, N.

The working of the movement is as follows :—Suppose the mechanism to be in the phase shown in the drawing; the wheel, L, is turning in the direction indicated by the arrow, and it will soon begin to pull the rod, K, upwards. Thus the disk or pawl plate, O O, is caused to revolve to a certain extent in the direction of the hands of a clock, and as it carries with it the pawl, M, that reaches, by the end of the stroke, another tooth of the ratchet wheel, which is all this time held immovable by the other pawl, N. But just before the end of the stroke, and before the pawl, M, has passed the fresh tooth of the ratchet wheel, the peg, P, also carried on the pawl plate, is brought into contact with the locking pawl, N, which it lifts out of the groove in the smaller ratchet wheel. Then the rod, L, begins to descend again; the pawl plate, o o, revolves in the opposite direction; the pawl, M, abuts against the fresh tooth of the larger ratchet wheel, and forces it round one-sixth of a revolution. That is the end of its stroke, and at that instant the locking pawl, N, being no longer held up by the peg, P, which has retreated, slips into the fresh groove of the smaller ratchet wheel and locks the whole thing, bringing the mechanism again into the phase indicated in the drawing.

The " Ratchet and Pawl Spring Escapement."

Suppose a ratchet wheel to be loosely placed upon a spindle, so that it is free to turn upon it; then suppose it to be attached to the spindle by means of a spiral spring wound upon the latter, so that the spindle will turn to a certain extent even when the wheel is held stationary by a pawl, and in doing so, of course, winds up the spring; then, when the pawl is lifted from the teeth of the ratchet wheel, that wheel will fly round rapidly until the spring is unwound again as before.

This is the principle of the movement of one of the successful cinematographs. It is shown diagrammatically in fig. 8, where the shaded portion represents, as before, that part of the mechanism which derives intermittent motion from the continuously moving parts which are shown blank. In this diagram, K and E are respectively two ratchet wheels, each of six teeth, but the teeth of one are turned in the opposite direction to those of the other. The inner one, K, is connected directly with the spindle, and it is turned continuously, for it is in actual connection with the handle of the instrument. The other one, E, fits loosely upon the same spindle, to which it is joined by means of a spiral spring, not shown in the sketch, one end of which is fastened to the spindle, while the other is attached to the wheel, E.

The two ratchet wheels would turn together upon the spindle as if they were one piece, were it not for the pawl, N:

but this engages firmly with one of the teeth of the larger
wheel, and as the smaller one is turned, therefore the
spring upon the spindle tightens up and increases the
tendency of the larger ratchet wheel to turn as soon as it is
released by the pawl. This release is periodically accomplished in the manner which will be plain from the diagram.
Attached to the pawl is a contact plate extended above the
larger ratchet wheel to rest against the teeth of the smaller.
As this latter turns continuously, it acts the part of a cam,
and pushes back the pawl six times in every revolution.

As soon as the pawl looses its hold upon it, the larger

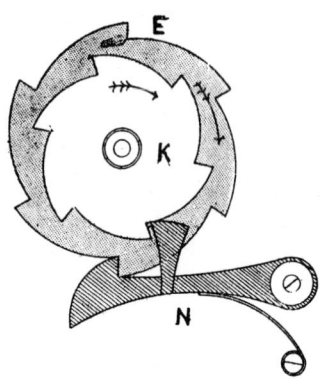

Fig. 8.

ratchet wheel spins round by virtue of the coiled spring
one-sixth of a turn. By that time the six-sided cam has
ceased to lift the pawl, which therefore drops back into
place, and, catching in the next tooth of the ratchet wheel,
brings it to rest again.

The sprocket wheel is attached to the larger ratchet
wheel directly; so that derives the necessary intermittent
motion by means of a singularly compact piece of mechanism
direct from the continuously turning spindle upon which it
is mounted. It may be thought a weak point in this
principle that the mechanism constructed upon it must be
very liable to wear, especially owing to the continuously
recurring collisions between the teeth of the ratchet wheel

and the edge of the pawl. But where these parts are made of steel—as they certainly should be—this wear is not very rapid; and even when it does occur, it is not of a nature to interfere with the working of the instrument until the teeth are worn down to a very considerable extent. It simply means that as the instrument gets old the wheel will turn a little farther round than it used to, but the amount of escapement will still be a sixth of a revolution every time. The picture will appear a little higher or a little lower on the screen than it would if the teeth were not at all worn away; but that is a very easy matter to compensate, for all machines are necessarily fitted with an adjustment for this error.

The " Broken Screw " Movement.

One of the first things that a mechanic has to learn when he is set to work at the lathe is how to cut a screw thread by hand. The " work " to be operated upon is placed between the lathe centres, and turned up true. To cut the screw thread upon it, a tool, called a comb or " chaser," is pressed against it as it turns, and at the same time slowly moved along in the direction of its length. This " chaser " is like a rack cut on the end of a piece of steel—simply a series of grooves cut in a peculiar manner. Naturally, if the forward motion of the tool be regular and duly proportioned in speed to the rate at which the work is turning, the teeth will cut into the material with the result of forming around it a screw thread. It is not a very easy thing to do, and the earlier results of the workman are always more or less " wobbly," as he himself would technically term them.

Suppose a " wobbly," or " drunken," thread of this kind to be purposely cut upon a cylinder, and that the screw thus formed be rotated in contact with the edge of a tangent wheel; the slow, rotary motion which would thus be imparted by the former to the latter would then be alternately slow and fast if the screw be turned regularly. And if the screw be so very " drunken " that it is only progressive at one portion of its circumference, and at all

3

others it is simply so many parallel grooves cut around the cylinder at right angles to its length, the tangent wheel would receive no motion at all when this portion of the screw is in engagement with it, but would only turn when the progressive portion of the thread comes round: in other words, the motion which it would derive from the screw would be intermittent.

That is the outline of a principle that has been adapted to cinematograph construction. As may be supposed, the original idea of a " drunken " screw and tangent wheel of

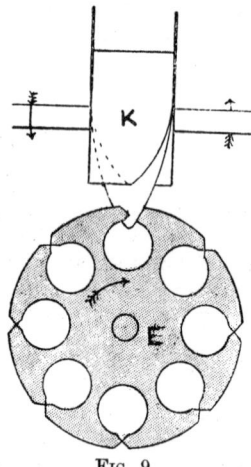

Fig. 9.

the pattern which might be imagined from this description had to be considerably modified to suit the exigencies of so exacting a piece of mechanism as a cinematograph. The form which the movement generally takes is described in the diagram (fig 9). The thick tangent wheel, with the screw grooves cut in its hollow rim, has given place to a circular disc with a few slots cut at regular intervals in its edge. In the present case the wheel has eight such slots, for it is designed to actuate an " eight-picture " sprocket wheel, and these slots are, for convenience sake, cut into eight circular holes pierced in the disk.

In the same way the worm wheel has been subjected to similar modification. The "pitch" of the screw—the distance from one thread to another—is equal to the distance between the slots on the tangent wheel, and only one complete convolution of the worm is retained, all the rest being dispensed with. The thread takes a peculiar form, too, and the diameter of the screw is very large. In the diagram, к is the screw, and it will be seen to be more like a spool or reel than what is generally understood as a screw. It is like a barrel with a broad rim at either end, but at one side the rim breaks away from one end and crosses over to the other, and then, continuing parallel to the ends of the barrel, forms the other rim. It continues round the barrel as a parallel rim until it gets opposite that point where it broke away from the other side, and at this point it comes to an abrupt termination. In the same way, the other rim only commences at the point where, at its other extremity, it joins the rim opposite.

I am afraid that this is not a very clear description, but then, this "broken screw" is not at all an easy thing to describe. I hope the drawing will make the matter clearer.

The worm, к, is continuously turning at the rate of one revolution per picture. For the greater part of its revolution the two parallel rims are inserted in two proximate slots on the tangent wheel, and thus hold it firmly locked and immovable. When that part of the worm comes round at which the thread crosses from one extremity to the other, one parallel rim comes to an abrupt end, and. thus leaves the tangent wheel at the mercy of the ot er The other immediately crosses over in a curved, inclined plane to the opposite end of the cylinder, and, in doing so, of course carries with it the edge of the tangent wheel, which is thus turned upon its axis to the extent of one-eighth of a revolution—equivalent to one picture's length of the sprocket wheel. Directly this movement is completed, and the worm, having crossed from one side to the other of the cylinder, becomes parallel again, the other parallel edge inserts itself into a fresh slot on the rim of the tangent wheel, and so it continues as long as the worm wheel continues to revolve.

This " broken screw " method involves an excellent principle for the transformation of continuous into intermittent motion for cinematograph purposes, but as usual it has its disadvantages. These are found in the great mechanical difficulties to be met with in the making of that irregular screw with the necessary precision, and in accurately shaping and bevelling the slots into which the worm fits. The result is, that the movement is either an expensive one to make, or it is so inefficient that it is extremely noisy, and does not, withal, yield satisfactory results.

As in so many other cases, the whole question resolves itself into one of good or bad workmanship. If the mechanism be really well worked out and accurately accomplished, the instrument may give results which could hardly be beaten by any of its rivals. If, on the other hand, the mechanism be inefficiently carried out, the results will be bad in every way. But that is true of every mechanical device that has ever been applied to the requirements of cinematography.

CHAPTER V.

CONTINUOUS MECHANISM.

AND now we come to the second great class of instruments for the projection of the living photographs upon the lantern screen. Hitherto those have only been considered in which the intermittent motion of the film is imparted to it directly by the intervention of mechanism which moves intermittently. But it was mentioned at the time that there is also another great category of machines in which the motion of every portion of the mechanism was either continuous or reciprocal, while, at the same time, the film was made to leap forward with the necessary jerky motion.

Strangely enough, both the pioneer machines in this class are of French design. The English people do not appear to have grasped the fact that the film may be made to move in the desired series of jerks by mechanism whose motion is not intermittent. Now there are several instruments which may be included in this class, but many of them are copies of either one or the other of the systems presently to be described.

The "Claw" Movement.

In an earlier chapter reference was made to the "one-hole" system of film perforation that had been adopted and the method of punching the holes in the film was described and illustrated. The numerous perforations in the Edison, or "four-hole," system were, it will be remembered, for the purpose of giving to the picture strip a firm grasp upon the rollers by which it was

hauled through the instrument, and the rollers were fitted
with a corresponding number of pegs to engage in the
perforations. Where a system is found in which those
numerous perforations are absent, it may be moderately
safely concluded that the toothed rollers, or "sprocket
wheels," are absent also.

According to the "one-hole" system of perforation (*see*
fig. 2) there is one small hole on either side of each picture.
In the cinematograph for which the pictures are intended,
a little claw with two nails, as it were, grasps the film by
means of those two holes into which it inserts itself; draws
it down the required distance, and then withdraws; jumps
up to the next pair of holes, and pulls the film down another
picture's length, and so on.

It might not, at first sight, appear that this is a very
good system by which to impart to the film the intermittent
motion that is so necessary for the purpose in view.   It
might seem that to obtain the required reciprocating
motion of the little claw would involve the employment of
some very complex mechanism ; and that, supposing the
movement to be satisfactorily obtained, the effect upon the
film would not be such as to yield a very steady picture
upon the screen, while it would be particularly liable to
tear the pellicle.

These objections are easily disposed of. It is easy to
make the pegs of the reciprocating "claw" to fit the holes
in the film so accurately that they are even less liable to
tear the film than the sprocket wheel movements that have
already been described, while the movements of the pellicle
are, in the well-made instruments, so perfectly unrestrained
and easy that only the minimum of strain is applied to it
by the intermittent tugs of the little claw. As to the
mechanism by which the motion is obtained, it is perhaps
rather more complex than many of those that have been
alluded to, but of that the reader will have an opportunity of judging from the appended description.   In the
instruments under consideration the workmanship is so
perfect, and every detail so excellently carried out and
beautifully made, that the machinery runs as smoothly as
if it were of the simplest description. And as to the
steadiness of the picture upon the screen, and the general

excellence of the results, it is quite unnecessary to speak, for the instrument has already earned for itself so world-wide a reputation.

The mechanical principle involved in this, what I have called the " claw," movement is very difficult to describe

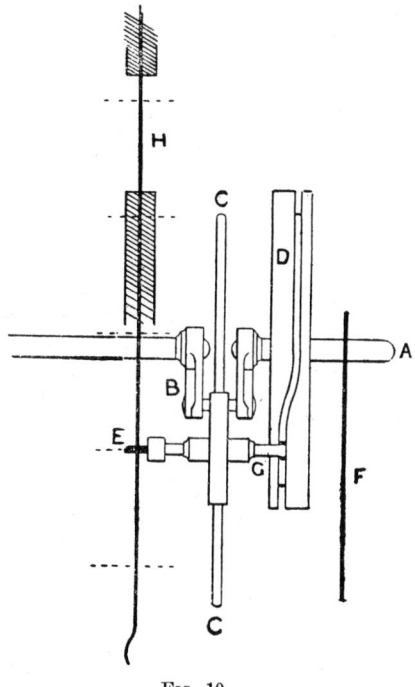

Fig. 10.

—a fact that may perhaps be ascribed to the somewhat unusually complex nature of the mechanism. Imagine either a cam or a crank so arranged as to impart to a sliding frame an up-and-down motion with every turn of the shaft, the frame being so fitted with guide rods and bearings that it can only move in this one plane. Then suppose that upon the same shaft is fitted another cam,

working at right angles to the former, and at alternate
periods. In the frame which moves up and down at the
instance of the first-mentioned cam let there be a smaller
sliding frame capable of movement at right angles to it;
then, if this latter frame be arranged so that it is actuated
by the second cam, it will move around the sides of a
square or oblong. In a sense, the circle will have been
squared, for the circular movement of the shaft will have
been transformed into such a movement of the little frame
that it will describe a square in its passage.

All of which I can hardly hope is understandable as it
is. Perhaps with the aid of a diagram (fig. 10) I shall be
able to make my meaning clearer. In the drawing, A
is the main shaft of the instrument, which is turned at the
necessary rate—say, fifteen revolutions per second, for one
picture is changed at every turn—by means of a handle,
to which it is connected by gear wheels to give it the
necessary speed. B is a crank by which up-and-down
motion is communicated to the frame carrying the pins
or "claw," which is restricted absolutely to this up-and-
down path by the guide rods, C and C, running in guides
which are not shown in the drawing. This frame carries
a short tube, in which the rod, G, is free to move to and fro,
that is to say, in a direction at right angles to that in
which the frame moves. At the right-hand end of this
rod, as you look at the sketch, is a little block of steel,
which fits into the groove cut in the periphery of a large
wheel, seen edgewise, as it were, at D. This wheel is
pivoted on the same shaft as that which bears the crank,
and obviously, if that groove were simply turned true on
its edge, it would communciate no sort of motion to the
little block of steel, G; and the claw, E (only one pin of
which is visible in the sketch), would simply travel up and
down under the influence of the crank.

But the groove on the wheel, D, is not straight. At
two places on the circumference of the wheel it bends : one
bend shifts it from one side of the edge of the wheel to the
other, as shown in the drawing; and the other bend—on
the opposite side of the wheel—shifts it back again. So it
will be seen that the little block, G, being free to move
from right to left, and *vice versâ*, gets that motion imparted

to it from this erratic groove, for in that groove its head is always buried.

Now I think it will be plain what effect the combination of those two motions must have upon the little pegs or " claw," E. This claw gets an up-and-down motion or " stroke " of about five-eighths of an inch from the crank, and at the end of each stroke—at the " dead centres," as it were—it gets a very rapid in-and-out motion from the twisted groove of the big wheel, an *in* push just after the up stroke, and an *out* pull after the down stroke.

The thick black vertical line towards the left-hand side of the sketch represents the film as seen from the edge. It passes between the usual guides to keep it at the focal point, and these are cut away at the position marked H, in a little window from which the picture is projected by the lens system upon the screen. Some perpendicular dotted lines crossing it at regular intervals indicate the position of the perforations—one on either side of each little picture.

It will be apparent that when the instrument is in the phase shown in the drawing, the claw is inserted in one pair of perforations and the little picture is in its proper position at the window, H. The shaft, A, is designed to be turned in the direction of the hands of a clock, if viewed from the end shown at the left-hand side : that is to say, looking at the instrument as it is shown in the sketch, the upper edge of the shaft and wheels is supposed to be turning towards you.

As the crank, B, is evidently at its lowest point, continued movement must necessarily tend to raise it. But with respect to the frame, C, the crank is at its dead centre at present ; and before any movement of the latter would have apparent effect upon the frame, the wheel, D, will have come into such a position that the rod, G, will have been withdrawn by the twisted groove on the circumference of the wheel, and the claw will have been made to release its hold upon the film. Therefore, as the frame carrying the claw rises up under the influence of the crank, the film will be left motionless, for there will be no influence tending to disturb its position as held and clamped between the guides which keep it in the projection plane.

Then, as soon as the little claw reaches the top of its
stroke, and thereby comes exactly opposite another pair of
perforations, it comes to rest owing to the crank having
reached the dead centre, and at the same time the twisted
groove on the big wheel slips back again into its former
position, pushes the claw forward into the holes in the film,
ready to drag it down one picture's length as soon as the
crank begins to descend.

So it will be seen that the movement is not so very complex after all. It has very many great advantages. The
machine runs as quietly as any machine on the market,
but that is chiefly owing to the excellence of the workmanship, which has already been mentioned. As a little
consideration will make evident, the movement of the film
is admirable, for the intermittent motion is not suddenly
applied to it, and it does not stop with a sudden jerk, as in
some of the movements that have been described. The
jerk begins gradually, reaches its greatest speed at the
middle of the stroke, and then its coming to rest is also
gradual. Also, the film does not rely upon the pressure of
the guide plates to arrest its motion at the end of the
periods of movement, for the little claw ends its downward
stroke before it is withdrawn from the holes in the film.
That is probably the chief reason of the wonderful steadiness
which is always noticeable with this machine.

To refer once more to the diagram (fig. 10), it should be
mentioned that the shutter, whose duty it is to cover up the
window at all those times when the film is moving, is shown
at F. It is in the form of a spread fan, and is mounted on
the main shaft. As the sketch represents the instrument
at one of the periods when the film is at rest, the shutter
is in such a position that it does not interfere with the projection of the picture upon the screen. As soon as the
crank bearing the little claw has made its upward stroke,
and the claw has been inserted in the film again, preparatory
to pulling it down with it, the shutter will come between
the lens and the picture aperture, so that the picture on
the screen is covered with a moment of darkness while the
film moves the required distance to bring a fresh phase of
the animated photograph into position.

Quite lately there has been introduced a modification of the " claw " principle, by which the mechanism is much simplified, and the instrument can therefore be made at a lower cost. In this instrument the motion applied to the claw by the mechanism is simply an up-and-down motion. The teeth of the claw are curved downwards, as shown in

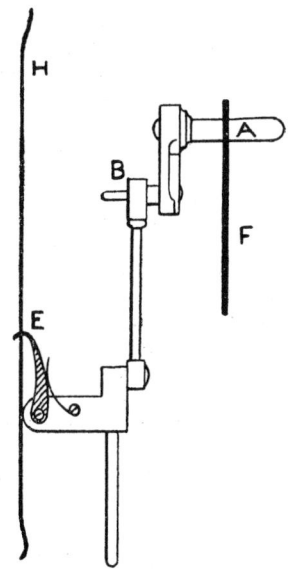

FIG. 11.

the sketch (fig. 11), and it is hinged and set against a very weak spring, so that slight pressure is sufficient to force it backwards. At the beginning of each downward movement the little claw slips into the two holes in the film which are immediately opposite it. It draws the film down to the full extent of its stroke, which is of course the required distance to make the new photograph exactly take the place of its predecessor, and then the upward stroke begins.

As the film is somewhat firmly held between the "pressure plates" it is easier for the little claw to "sit back," as it were, on its haunches, or rather springs, than to force the film up again with it. Accordingly, it does so, and does not come forward again until it reaches the top of its stroke and finds another pair of holes ready for it. The movement is extremely simple; and as the instrument that I saw was decidedly well made—which I have already said is perhaps the most important thing of all—it certainly worked remarkably well. Moreover, the teeth of the claw being sufficiently small, the instrument will work equally well with the "one-hole" or "four-hole" pictures, which, it is easy to see, is a strong point in its favour.

The " Dog " Movement.

It is an easy transition from a movement whose chief characteristic is a kind of feline "claw" to that which I have called the "dog" movement, from the fact that the film receives its intermittent motion from an eccentric very like the "dog" on a turning lathe. It has been said that these instruments of continuously moving mechanism are chiefly represented by two great systems, and the "cat's-claw" and the "dog" movements are the ones that I had in my mind's eye. Both, as has also been remarked, hail originally from France—indeed, rumour has it that on the Continent the two systems lead a veritable cat-and-dog kind of existence, so to speak, as they greedily contend with one another for the dainty bone of public recognition or popularity.

First let me describe, for the benefit of those who may happen not to know, just what is meant by the "dog" of a turning lathe. It consists of a solid metal wheel with a long peg projecting from its face near the edge. As the lathe turns, this peg revolves around the centre like a planet around the sun. Its object is to impart the necessary rotary motion to the "work" which is set between the lathe centres, and to this end it abuts against a carrier or artificial projection upon the work.

Suppose you hold a strip of "kinefilm" in contact with a "dog" while the lathe is in motion; the dog, as it turns,

will inflict a series of taps upon the surface of the film,
imparting a kind of alternate pull-and-let-go motion to
its ends. Now, arrange a sprocket wheel at one side of
the dog in such a manner that, turning slowly, it will
draw the film along to the extent of one picture at every
revolution of the lathe centre. The sprocket wheel turns
continuously, and draws the film continuously, but as it

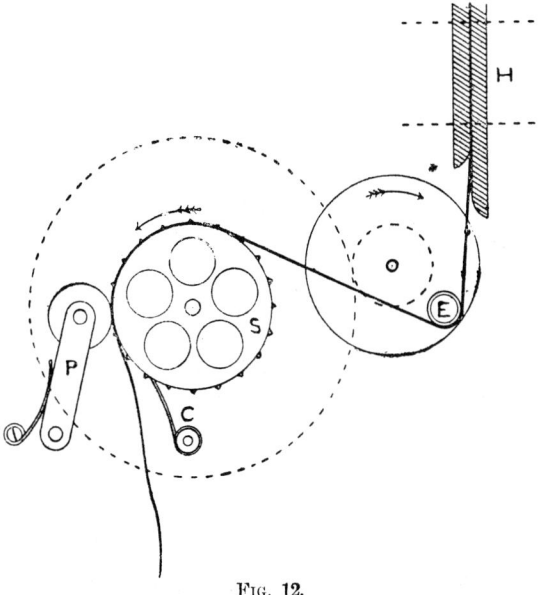

Fig. 12.

has to pass over the eccentric " dog," the continuous motion
is turned into intermittent jerks. Every time the dog has
a tug at it, as it were, it moves forward suddenly to the
required distance, and then remains at rest, while the dog
retires for a time, and the sprocket wheel steadily draws in
the slack that it has caused in the film.

That is the principle of the " dog " movement, and it has
the merit of extreme simplicity, as may be imagined.
Fig. 12 shows the arrangement in diagrammatic form as

applied to the requirements of cinematography. At H are
the pressure plates, whose duty it is to hold the film at
the projection point, at the correct focal distance from the
objective lens; and they are, of course, pierced with an
opening of the usual size to form a window, through which
the light gains access to the picture, and passes through it
to the screen. Then it passes under the eccentric, E, which,
as will be seen, is close to the edge of a wheel rather larger
than the sprocket wheel, and whose direction of revolution
is indicated by the arrow. Thence it passes around the
"five-picture" sprocket wheel, which, turning continuously,
draws it steadily forward. The rest, little as it is, consists
merely of accessories. Thus P is a pressure roller requisite
to hold the film in sufficiently intimate contact with the
sprocket wheel; and C is a scraper, whose duty it is to
dissolve that connection when it has gone on long enough
to serve the required purpose, and to peel off the film and
start it on its journey to the receiving basket or spool, as
the case may be.

In the drawing, the sprocket wheel and the eccentric are
connected together by gear wheels, the larger one five
times the size of the other; and these are indicated in the
sketch by dotted circles. By this arrangement the "dog"
is forced to make five attacks upon the film for every one
revolution of the sprocket wheel—or once for each picture.
Upon the size and position of this "dog," with reference to
the sprocket wheel and the pressure plates, from between
which the film is fed to it, the speed with which one
picture is changed to the next entirely depends. In an
instrument with which I have often worked, and which gives
very satisfactory results in my hands, the proportions and
positions of the various parts are very much as shown in
the sketch, and with this arrangement the change from one
picture to the next occupies half the time that it is stationary:
that is to say, of the total time occupied in the showing of
an animated photograph with this machine, rather less
than one-third is taken up by the movement of the film
while it is stationary, and its image is being projected upon
the screen for the remaining two-thirds. In another
machine worked upon the same principle, but rather differently carried out, the period of movement bears to that

of rest a relation of one in six. With such a machine the size of the shutter may be very much reduced, with the result that the picture on the screen is much more brilliant, while the flickering of the light is considerably diminished. But, on the other hand, it stands to reason that where the change has to be made in such a much shorter time, the film must necessarily move much faster, and the change from rapid motion to actual rest much more abrupt. Consequently, whatever liability there is in the slower machine to tear or damage the film must be very much increased. I must say, however, that in the course of a pretty long experience with an instrument built on the principle I have indicated, I do not find it at all more liable to damage the pellicle than the majority of others. But this question of the liability of the films to damage under differing conditions is one of great importance, for their cost is a very serious item in the general bill of expenditure, and it may well be left for consideration in a more favourable place.

The " Epicycloidal " Movement.

Here is quite a different principle applied to the requirements of cinematography. In the machines built upon this new principle we find a sprocket wheel which not only revolves continuously upon its own axis, but at the same time waltzes bodily around a fixed point at some little distance from its centre. That is to say, its manner of revolution is very much like that of a planet around its sun, except that its orbit is so much restricted that there would not be room for a centre luminary, no matter how small it might be. The manner in which this motion is obtained will be apparent from the drawing (fig. 13). As will be seen, the drum has a small cog-wheel on its axis which gears into another stationary one on the main axis of the instrument. As the wheel attached to the toothed cylinder is forced to revolve around the stationary wheel, it receives an independent rotary motion therefrom.

A little consideration will reveal the effect which this complex motion must have upon the film drawn by the sprocket wheel. Remember that the drum is turning on its axis *in the same direction* as that with which it revolves around the fixed point. The supply of film is from above, and when the sprocket wheel is both turning and descending, the two movements are combined to draw down the film at double pace. But when the opposite state of affairs is in progress, when the sprocket wheel, although still turning on its own axis, is rising or approaching the supply of film, the two actions exactly counteract one another, and the film at the window remains stationary: in fact, the

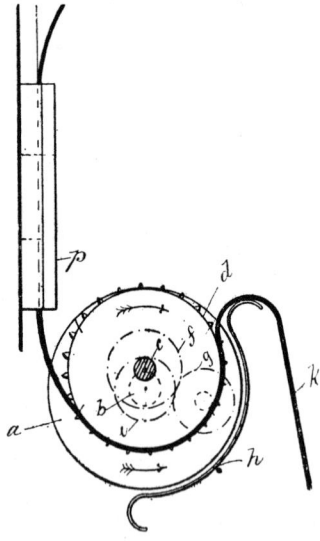

Fig. 13.

sprocket wheel simply rolls upwards along the loop of film, and does not move it. It is a movement which is extremely pretty to watch, and, complex as it may seem at first sight, it is really quite simple, and even if it were not so, the results which it yields are such as to justify considerable trouble in arriving at them.

In the drawing (fig. 13), A is a disc mounted on the end of the spindle, B, and it carries eccentrically the sprocket wheel, D, which is capable of revolving on the spindle, c.

On the end of the bearing on which spindle B revolves is a stationary gear wheel, E, and another gear wheel, F, is fixed to the sprocket wheel, D, the two being geared together by an intermediate wheel, G.

The "Intermittent Grip" Movement.

Here again we are introduced to quite a different

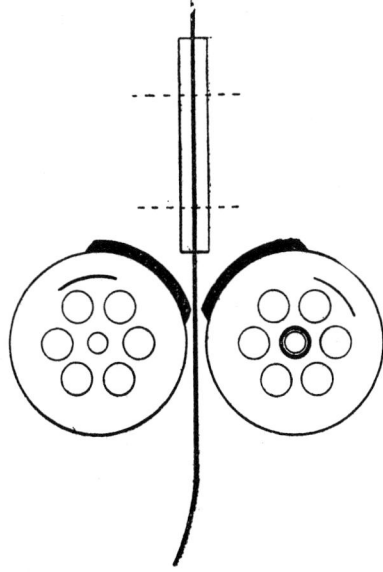

Fig. 14.

principle; and although, so far as I am aware, instruments based upon it are not on the general market, yet it is responsible for one of the most successful cinematographs that has yet been exhibited.

When you turn an ordinary roller mangle—only as an amateur, of course—the material which you place between the rollers is drawn through them steadily as you turn. But if the greater part of the surface of those rollers were

4

broken away, the stuff would only be gripped and drawn
through when two unbroken portions came opposite one
another—a state of things which would occur regularly,
and naturally result in transmitting an intermittent movement to the material between them. It would move
forward a step at a time, and each step would be equal.

In the diagram (fig. 14), the two rollers of a cinematograph on this principle are represented. Their surface is cut away all round in each case, except a portion
corresponding as exactly as possible to the dimensions of
one picture on the film between them. This film has no
perforations, and as it is practically impossible to so gauge the
exact length of a picture—and that has been shown to be a
variable quantity, depending on weather and other things—
a regulating device has to be provided. The necessary regulation is accomplished by hand, as the picture is watched
on the screen, by means of causing the little cheek on one
roller to lag very slightly behind the other : that is to
say, the roller is turned on its spindle very slightly while it,
spindle and all, is rapidly revolving.

The manner in which this seemingly difficult feat is
accomplished is very ingenious, but need not be entered
into here. The effect of causing one cheek to turn slightly
behind the other is to lessen the extent of the grip they
give to the film, therefore less of it is drawn through at a
time. Much of the beauty of the projected picture depends
upon the readiness and skill of him who has charge of the
regulating device ; and even in the most favourable cases the
picture is seen to slowly rise and fall to a small extent on the
screen. Beyond that, the projected photograph is remarkably steady.

Although by far the larger number of present-day instruments belong to the former of the two categories, into
which, as I have said, they can all be divided—that is to
say, they depend upon intermittently moving mechanism
to give the necessary intermittent motion to the film—and,
as has also been said, one class cannot claim any
superiority over the other, for there are good instruments
in each, there appears to be a growing tendency in favour
of the latter class. For my part, I cannot help thinking
the best machines of the future will be found among those

with the continuous mechanism; but up to the present writing it would not be fair to say that they have any demonstrable advantage over their more jerky brothers, and in point of numbers they are certainly in the minority. However, that is nothing, for there are many machines on the market which are thoroughly bad, and therefore need not be counted.

CHAPTER VI.

THE SHUTTER.

IT may safely be said that upon no part of the cinematograph does so much diversity of opinion exist as
upon the shutter.   Some people contend that the lens
should be absolutely covered during every instant that the
film behind it is in motion; others go so far as to say
that there is no need for any shutter at all.   Some seek a
middle course by making the shutter of some translucent
material, such as semi-opaque celluloid of a ground-glass
appearance; others pierce a few large holes in an opaque
shutter, while others, again, favour a number of small ones.
Then some carry it a step farther, and introduce perforated
zinc or wire gauze in their efforts to minimise the flicker,
without destroying the brilliancy of the effect upon the
screen.   Then some are in favour of segment shutters,
like that shown in fig. 15; while others like the cut-away
cylinder pattern, as in fig. 16.   Some serrate the edges;
some don't.   Many like it in front of the lens, while many
more say it should be behind, and many more still put
it between the film and the condenser.   And so each one
goes his own way, which is different from all the others.
But there is one common attribute of all classes of shutter
or no shutter—one tie which binds all systems together
in an indissoluble bond of brotherhood; and that is, that
each and every description of kind or shape or place or
absence of shutter is positively the only one that gives the
best results, and by its aid "the flicker so noticeable in
most machines," etc., etc.

But we, as unbiassed onlookers and recorder, may
attempt to analyse the various claims to excellence of the

different devices that have been brought forward to solve
this important question of the shutter. Important it
certainly is, for it is to the shutter that all the blame of
the flicker must be laid, and also a considerable portion of
the loss of light, which is such a serious matter to the
cinematograph.

Undoubtedly the best way to reduce the flicker in the
cinematograph as at present constructed—and it is a con-
summation devoutly to be wished, as every one will admit—
is to reduce its period to the least possible extent : that
is to say, to so arrange the shutter that it covers the lens
for as short a time as possible in comparison with the
period for which the light is allowed unimpeded progress.

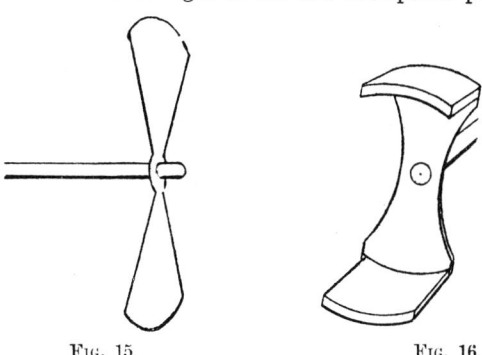

Fig. 15.   Fig. 16.

But as—theoretically, at all events—the shutter must
cover the lens at all such times as the film is in motion,
and only leave it uncovered when the picture is at rest,
we soon reach an unalterable limit, although the limit is
fixed at different points in the different systems of intermittent motion.

And then the question naturally arises, having reduced
the shutter to its smallest possible area, consistent with
the necessity of keeping the lens covered at all such times as
the film is in motion, is there any other means by which
the painful flickering can be further reduced or altogether
obviated ? As has already been hinted, that is a question
which would be answered differently by different individuals.

For a long time I was at a loss to account for this great diversity of opinion on what appeared to be a simple question, and one that could be easily settled by experiment; but I have recently been making a few experiments with a view to satisfying myself upon the point, yet have only succeeded in shaking my original conviction that, to secure the best all-round results, an opaque shutter was necessary, without being able to form any fresh opinion as to what really is the best form of shutter. It appears to me that the reason for all this diversity of opinion is this : different forms of shutter are suitable for different classes of picture.

It is granted that the shutter is the cause of the flicker which every cinematograph experimenter is trying to get rid of. In the machine with which I made the few trials that I have spoken of, the period of darkness is about one-third the duration of that of light : that is to say, that the shutter—which is of the fan pattern—is a segment occupying 120° of the circle; in other words, it is a shutter of about the average duration, and therefore gives the average amount of flicker.

The flicker was particularly noticeable in one picture, which, as may be supposed, represented a mass of light with very little dark contrast. It is the pictures with the large clear white spaces that show the flicker to the greatest extent. The experiment was first tried of removing the shutter altogether, with highly satisfactory results : that is to say, that the flicker was altogether done away with ; and although there were vertical lines—technically called " rain "—above and below every clearly defined patch of dark shadow on the picture, these were so very faint as to be negligible. Then a picture subject was chosen in which there was one brilliant light patch in vivid contrast to a very dark background. The effect of projecting this film without a shutter can only be described as truly horrible. The light patch was drawn out into a vertical white band spreading right over the background, and indeed entirely blotting it out above and below. Ordinary pictures, neither of a very light description, nor of this highly contrasted kind, took up a position midway between these extremes, but in almost every case the faults

introduced by the removal of the shutter were great enough
to more than counterbalance the gain in the absence of
flicker.   In an ordinary street scene, for instance, each
moving figure would be seen to be followed about wherever
it moved by a storm of "rain," as if directed by an
avenging providence in retribution for its jerky gait.
The appearance is not natural—although many a man who
has left his umbrella at home on a showery day will be
ready to swear that the rain does follow him about in this
manner.

Then it was sought to overcome the difficulty by splitting
the difference.   A shutter of translucent material was
placed in the position of the opaque one, and it was supposed that this would allow a large quantity of light to
reach the screen in the intervals between the pictures, and
thus do away with the flicker, while it would so obliterate
detail by dispersion of the light as to make the "rain"
effect invisible.   In reality the dispersion of the light is
such that it illuminates the whole room in a series of flashes,
which, blending into one another by " persistence of vision,"
give the effect of a lantern show in a room that is not
properly darkened.   The screen is illuminated between the
pictures by a period of semi-light in place of the period of
darkness that would obtain if an opaque shutter were
employed.   Consequently the flicker is very much reduced,
but, owing to that " persistence of vision" which makes
animated photographs possible, the impression of light upon
the retina stays there through the succeeding picture, and
fogs it with a flood of grey mist that blocks out all the
brilliancy.   In my opinion, at all events, the last state is
worse than the first: the fog is more objectionable than
the flicker.

Another method is to pierce the shutter with one or two
holes, so that a few rays of light get through to break the
period of darkness.   By this plan the flicker is undoubtedly
reduced, and the picture gains proportionately in brightness.
With the majority of films the result is a decided improvement, and in the considerable number that I have tried
under these conditions, I have not found one that had
such extensive defects introduced by it that it must be
regarded as undesirable.   In certain trying cases, as, for

instance, in that of a dancer with a very white dress, there is a tiresome repetition of the main points of the picture above and below the correct position—one, indeed, for each perforation in the shutter; but unless the perforations be unduly large, this "mirage" effect is not sufficiently pronounced to be really objectionable.

So, it will be seen, the whole question resolves itself into the statement that certain films admit of a different degree of perforation without involving the introduction of a detrimental amount of "ghost," or blur, or other faults. As it is hardly feasible to alter the degree of permeability for every film that is passed through the machine, the simplest plan is to hit upon a fair average and stick to it. After the experiments that I have hinted at, and as a result, I decided upon cutting four slits in my shutter, each occupying about 7° or 8° of arc, and equidistant from one another; and I have seen no cause to regret the decision. It must not be supposed for a moment, however, that I have any idea of presuming such a shutter is best: but it has proved so in my hands, and, possibly, it may serve as some slight guide to other experimenters. The shutter—using the word to convey the impression that a period of darkness or semi-darkness is introduced to cover the change from one little picture to the next—is undoubtedly the cause of flicker; and as it is only reasonable to suppose that experimenters will never rest until flicker has been abolished in connection with cinematography, it is pretty safe to say that in the instrument of the future the shutter will not be found. Beyond that mild prophecy it would be but rash to venture.

There is one little matter closely connected with the shutter which it would be well to mention before leaving the subject, and that is the question of vibration : not the vibration of the picture in its frame on the screen—for that is merely a matter of good films and good workmanship in the instrument; but vibration of the whole machine, picture frame and all, by which the whole projected image is seen to vibrate on the screen quite independently of, and added to, its own inherent unsteadiness. This is almost always caused by the shutter, and exhibits itself in lack of definition, or "fuzziness," on the screen. When the living photograph has the appearance of a photographic product of a Salonic disciple of Astigmatism, it is only natural in the uninitiated to blame the objective lens with which the picture is projected. In many cases, however, the fault is not with the lens at all, but simply with the vibration of the image. A fan-shaped shutter, with its axis parallel to the optical axis of the instrument, may not be truly counterbalanced—and it is wonderful how little preponderence on one side will cause a great deal of vibration when the shutter is rapidly turned; and this communicates a small lateral shake to the whole machine, or possibly to the front lens only, and draws the detail of the projected picture into lateral lines, so that it looks as if it were out

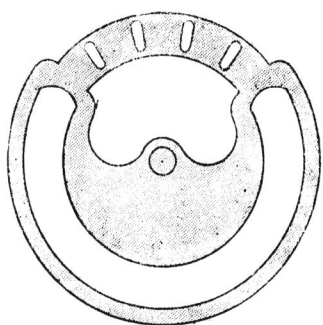

FIG. 17.

of focus. Or a cylindrical shutter may act in the same way—though it is not so liable to the fault; and as its axis is at right angles to that of the instrument, it causes it to shake up and down, and the definition is distorted vertically. The remedy is, of course, to remove the shutter, and carefully counterbalance it, or file it away, until, when accurately poised, it will remain in any position without showing the least tendency to revolve.

It may be taken almost as an axiom that, no matter what description of shutter is used, it should be as light as possible. Very thin alluminium, cut away wherever possible to reduce the weight, but, of course, accurately counterbalanced, is perhaps the best material to use.

Many an instrument that gives unsatisfactory results now might be immensely improved by detaching its present shutter, and replacing it with one of thin alluminium or even of paper,—and paper will make a very good shutter, for the centrifugal force will keep it straight and rigid when in use.

Fig. 17 shows the form of shutter that I have found to work excellently. It is cut out of thin sheet alluminium, and the openings are arranged in such a manner that an equivalent amount of material is removed at the openings on either side, and no attached counterweight is necessary. It weighs but an ounce or so, and does not in any way affect the steadiness of the picture. I merely mention it in the hope that the hint may possibly be of use to others who possess machines in which the vibration caused by the shutter interferes with the good definition of the projected picture.

CHAPTER VII.

ILLUMINANTS: THE LIMELIGHT.

A SHORT consideration of the conditions under which the living photographs are projected upon a lantern screen will speedily reveal the fact that it is by no means easy to obtain a sufficiently brilliant light to exhibit them properly except upon a very small scale. The optical arrangements of a cinematograph are rather more like those of a lantern microscope than those which obtain in an ordinary lantern, and everybody knows how difficult, indeed impossible, it is to secure adequate illumination for that instrument except for very small pictures. For living photograph projection the conditions are, of course, not anything like so stringent as those which must be faced before an exhibition with the projection microscope can be undertaken, but they are far more exacting than those which pertain to the ordinary lantern.

In the first place the degree of magnification of a cinematograph picture is about nine times that of an ordinary lantern picture ; and although an attempt is made to concentrate the same amount of light on the smaller slide, that can never be successfully accomplished unless, indeed, our opticians turn their attention successfully to the construction of a special condenser for cinematograph work. There is, then, a considerable loss of light, on account of the small size of the picture and the great extent to which it has to be magnified. That is loss No. 1. Then there is the shutter. The amount of light which this cuts off varies very considerably in machines on different systems, as has already been explained ; for some shutters keep the lens covered during just as long periods as those in which it is open, while others only cover it a sixth of this time, and even then allow part of the light to pass through. The merits and demerits of the different schemes of shutters have already been discussed. Let it be granted that the shutter on an average cuts off a third of the light which would otherwise reach the screen. That is loss No. 2. And the third account on which loss of light inevitably occurs is the fact that celluloid is not so transparent as glass.

But difficulties, they say, were made to be overcome. By the careful choice of suitable lenses—condensers and objectives carefully selected and wedded to one another in view of the special conditions under which they have to work—one source of loss can be considerably minimised. Again, by so arranging the mechanism that the period of rest of the film is very considerably longer than the time in which it is moving, so that it is only necessary for the shutter to obscure the light for a comparatively short period; and even by piercing the shutter, and rendering it translucent, so that while it covers the lens it does not altogether shut off the light, difficulty No. 2 assumes its smallest proportions. And as to the transparency of the films, that is a matter which is under the control of two bodies. There is the maker of the celluloid, and he has already made his product remarkably transparent; and there is the photographer, who is beginning to learn the great importance of transparency and the non-necessity of more than quite a small degree of density, but he does not always live up to his convictions. However, wonderful improvements have been made in this respect during the last few months, and there is every reason to suppose that in a short time commercial cinematographic films will be as good in their way as the best lantern slides on the market.

To quote another proverb, "Every cloud has a silver lining." And the gloom which has been cast, literally and figuratively, over the art of cinematography by the difficulties that the light in the lantern has to encounter before it reaches the sheet, shows us its silver lining in the good service it has done, and is still doing, to the art of lantern projection generally. Only to mention one instance, because it happens to come under the special domain of this chapter, the difficulties of securing adequate illumination for cinematographs has led to remarkable improvements in the manufacture of limelight apparatus, which cannot fail to be a lasting benefit to lanternists of all denominations long after cinematography has had its day.

It does not come within the scope of this very unpretending little manual to give instructions in the use of the limelight, and hints for its manipulation in connection with the cinematograph. The manner of employing it for the projection of the living photographs differs in no way from its use for ordinary lantern work, and full particulars and directions are to be found in any good text-book on the lantern. But as there will possibly be many lovers of the lantern who have hitherto been content with a specimen of the oil-lit variety, and who may now be desirous of adding a few cinematograph pictures to their collection, I may just make two suggestions for their benefit.

In the first place, if they be thinking of attaching a cinematograph to their present oil-light lantern, let me say at once, don't. Neither oil, acetylene, nor incandescent gaslight are of any practical use with a cinematograph. Not only is each very far from being brilliant enough, but the luminous area is in each case far too large. In the second place, if a consideration of possible danger in connection with the limelight deter you from its use, put that consideration behind you : the danger does not exist. That is speaking, of course, of the limelight in its up-to-date form. In the old days of gas bags and home-made oxygen, danger there was, as was abundantly and most unfortunately proved. Also in the early days of the compressed gas system there were a few accidents, but these were almost all traced to their source, and the cause removed. I do not think that with modern oxy-hydrogen apparatus the veriest bungler *could* negotiate an explosion even if he tried. One cannot say that of any kind of oil lantern, and acetylene must also stand aside for the present until it has been brought to a greater pitch of perfection.

But one thing must be borne in mind in connection with cinematographs and danger, and that is the extreme inflammability of the film pictures. The celluloid may take fire, and easily, too, from the concentrated heat from

the lime or arc light focussed upon it by the condenser, or
it may become accidentally ignited by a spark from a
match, or from the carbon points in the case of the electric
light, or more easily still by a piece of incandescent lime
dropping from the jet.

And so systems of lantern illumination which are perfectly safe in connection with ordinary lantern projection
become at once invested with a certain amount of danger
when contemplated in conjunction with a cinematograph.
Thus the excellent and convenient oxy-ether light may be
regarded, when used properly and under proper conditions,
as a safe means of lantern illumination ; but it has just
sufficient element of uncertainty about it to make a careful operator shun it where the living photographs are
concerned.

But although this is not the place to enter into details
of limelight manipulation, it is an eminently suitable one
in which to call attention to recent improvements in limelight apparatus that tend to make it more efficient for
cinematograph purposes.   One of these is undoubtedly the
new " F.B. " high-power jet that I have tested very
thoroughly, and with which I am very much pleased.
As regards the actual jet itself, it is merely a further
improvement on lines that have already been laid down,
but the improvement is very marked.   It has a large
mixing chamber of good construction, by which the gases
are very thoroughly mixed before reaching the nozzle.
The result is that an immensely powerful light can be
secured with a complete absence of noise.   The maker of
this jet does not follow the too prevalent fashion of quoting
most exaggerated estimates of the candle power that it is
supposed to emit ; but I have tested it competitively against
the electric arc, and find that even against this light—
consuming a moderately small current—it is able to hold
its own without difficulty.   With a larger current of twelve
to fifteen ampères it is, of course, beaten ; and, under any
circumstances, the limelight can never be so efficient as
the electric light for optical projection, on account of the
much larger size of its luminous area.

One of the points on which many good lantern illumin-
ants fail when applied to the cinematograph is this : the

vibration, which is, so far, more or less an inseparable attribute of all these instruments, induces a sympathetic vibration in the all too flimsy support of the light source. Thus a limelight jet—especially when it is fitted with the large and therefore heavy mixing chamber that is essential to the best results—will "wiggle" terribly on its frail supporting pin, which is usually placed right at the back, as if specially designed to further such a result. Animated photographs are already far too prone to flicker under the best of circumstances, as no one will, I think, be inclined to dispute, and this unsteadiness of the light only makes matters very much worse. Indeed, it is probable that in many cases much of the flicker that is attributed to the

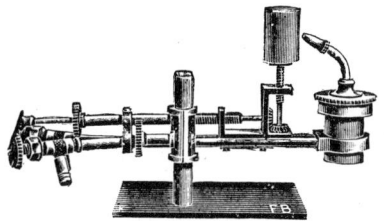

FIG. 18.

fault of the machine is, in reality, due to the unsteadiness of the limelight jet.

In the jet that I have just described (fig. 18) the designer has made a daring departure from the code of unwritten laws of jet construction, which are too often regarded as being as unalterable as those of the Medes and Persians. This departure has been made in the interests of the cinematograph, and affords another instance of the gratitude that is due from the ordinary lanternists to that instrument for the introduction of improvements in lighting apparatus of which he is bound to reap a large share of the benefit.

The improvement consists in replacing the usual tin tray by a solid base of sheet brass ; of shifting the pin from the back to the centre of the jet so that the weight which it has to support is more evenly distributed instead of being all at one side ; of making this pin about four times as thick as it would be under the older *régime*, and of replacing the horrible set screw for clamping the jet to the pin by a special grip that holds it absolutely firmly. A secondary advantage accrues from this new form of clamping device, and that is that the operation of centring the light—most important to be done accurately where cinematographs are concerned—is much facilitated ; for when the vice is slightly slackened, the collar slides smoothly over the pin, under the influence of a little pressure, in the required direction, and can be easily brought into position, when a touch of the clamping screw fixes it there immovably.

A good limelight jet, for cinematograph work, should have an ample mixing chamber, and be capable of yielding an intensely brilliant light without hissing or roaring. It should be so firmly clamped and supported in the lantern that it is impossible for it to vibrate, and the device by which it is centred in the optical system should be capable of accurate adjustment. The taps upon the jet should be smooth working, and may with advantage be of the fine adjustment variety, while a " Pringle cut-off " will be found of great benefit where the light has to be constantly extinguished and relighted.

CHAPTER VIII.

THE ELECTRIC ARC LIGHT.

ONE of the lasting benefits for which the lanternist of the future will be to a great extent indebted to the boom in living photographs is the popularisation of the electric arc light for lantern work. In the earlier days of cinematography, when the mechanism was poor and the films poorer still, the arc light was a positive necessity, for by no other means could sufficient illumination be secured to meet the exacting conditions under which alone the animated photographs were possible. And where electricity was a *sine quâ non*, operators who had hitherto fought shy of the new illuminant because they did not understand it were obliged to pocket their prejudices, and the result naturally was a number of converts to electricity for lanterns.

In the same way the objections of hall owners and others to the tapping of their mains for the benefit of the lanternist were soon overruled when it came to be a case of " it I will have, or you will have none "—meaning living photographs ; and it is only to be supposed that when once the lanternists and their like became familiar with the light, its many superiorities over any other form of illuminant for the purpose would speedily win for itself a place in their hearts.

Nowadays the cinematograph has been so much improved that the electric light is no longer a necessity ; but it is still, and always will be, a very great advantage. Not only is it far brighter than any other available illuminant, besides being quite as steady, and more convenient, reliable and efficient, but the extremely small size of the luminous area make it, optically speaking, much more perfect for projection work than any other. Unfortunately for its good fame, it occasionally gets handled by utterly incompetent and, indeed, foolish persons, and the idea has therefore very naturally gained credence among those who, by lack of knowledge, are unable to distinguish between a bad instrument and a good one in incompetent hands, that the light is unsatisfactory. And this deplorable result is also contributed to by the fact that ill-designed lamps are sometimes used, and, as may be supposed, yield a light which is unsteady and inefficient in every way. It is as obviously unfair to judge the system by such cases as it would be to condemn the limelight because an obsolete oxy-calcium (spirit) jet gives a poor and unsatisfactory light.

The increasing popularity which the electric light is daily gaining for cinematography, and the ever-increasing facilities for its use in places where but yesterday the necessary current was unobtainable, is sufficient excuse for a short chapter concerning it.

First as to the lamp—sometimes called a regulator—by which the electric current is converted into light. This is merely a device for holding the two carbons a certain distance apart, so that the electric current in jumping the gap between them shall develop sufficient heat to make their extremities glow with a brilliant incandescence. The effect of the heat upon the carbon is precisely the same as that of the oxy-hydrogen jet upon the lime—it makes it brilliantly white-hot; hence the light, and it causes it to gradually consume away. In the case of the lime, the supply has to be renewed as the substance is vapourised— which is easiest accomplished by turning the cylinder of lime round so that a new portion is presented to the action of the jet. And in the case of the carbons, their consumption is compensated for by "feeding" them closer together as they burn away.

In some of the earlier limelight jets a clockwork arrangement was attached, whose duty it was to turn the lime. In the same way, automatic regulators are obtainable by which the carbons of an arc lamp are brought together as they are consumed. As the "feeding" of the carbons by hand is no more arduous than the periodical turning of the lime, a "hand-feed" lamp is almost universally employed.

In an arc lamp working on the continuous current—as opposed to the "alternating" current, which will be mentioned presently—the two carbons consume at an unequal rate. That which is connected with the "positive" supply wire burns away at twice the rate of the "negative" carbon. It is usual to compensate for this by making the one of twice the sectional area of the other, so that they burn at equal rates—an arrangement that has other advantages, in that a better light is obtained by the use of a positive carbon that is larger than the negative.

In reality the light from the electric arc has three distinct sources. First, there is the glow from the "arc" itself—the stream of electricity across the space between the carbon points. This is of a purple hue, and is very faint compared to the others, and may be disregarded. Next in point of brilliancy is the glow from the incandescent tip of the negative carbon. It is a factor in the total illumination, but only a small one. By far the most brilliant of the three is the blaze of light which finds its source at the point of the positive carbon. At the end of this point a little hollow or "crater" is formed, and it is from the interior of this crater that the vast majority of the light streams.

With a view to inducing this little "crater" to always form quite in the centre of the end of the positive carbon, it is usual to employ a rod of hard carbon with a central core of softer material. This larger or "cored" carbon is placed in the upper arm or carbon holder of the lamp ; and with this arrangement, as may be supposed, practically all the light from the lamp is directed downwards, and forms a luminous area all around the smaller carbon rod. That is just what is required for ordinary illumination purposes, but for optical work all the light is wanted at one side.

To gain this end the upper (positive, cored) carbon is not placed exactly over its neighbour in the same straight line, but is drawn slightly behind it. The effect is to force the crater, which always forms opposite the nearest point of the negative carbon, to take up a position towards the front of the rod; and from here all its light is directed forwards, but still with a somewhat downward tendency. Then the whole arrangement, lamp and all, is tilted backwards about 15°, and thus the light issues in exactly the required direction.

I have said that the stream of electricity jumps across the space between the carbon points; it does this by virtue of the intensely heated carbon vapour which pervades that space, and which, being a partial conductor, makes the passage of the current across it possible. Before the light is started there is no such conducting vapour, and no light can be obtained until the presence of the vapour is secured. It is obtained by allowing the carbons to touch one another for a moment when the current is switched on, and then immediately separating them. The point of contact being insufficient to allow the large current of electricity to pass freely, some particles of carbon become intensely heated, give off the necessary vapour, and directly the points are separated the light is established. In technical parlance, this momentary touching of the carbons is called "striking the arc," and in practice a mere moment is sufficient. Owing to the absence of electric resistance between the carbons when they are in contact, the flow of current at that moment is very large. Therefore the contact should be made and broken as rapidly as possible, or the electrical arrangements may be seriously disturbed, and the supply possibly cut off altogether for the time being.

It is not proposed to enter here into the details of the electric conditions which must be observed in this connection, for that is a large subject, and has been fully treated elsewhere.* Sufficient will it be to give a few general directions for connecting up and operating an arc light in a lantern or cinematograph.

Electricity is usually supplied at an E.M.F. (electromotive force) of a hundred volts. That is its *pressure,*—regard it as the pressure on the gas supply to a limelight jet. You will have to reduce that to about forty-five or fifty volts by means of a "resistance,"—regard that as the regulator which reduces the pressure of the gas as it issues

* " The Electric Arc Light for Lantern Projection." By Cecil M Hepworth. Published by Messrs. Ross, Ltd.

from the cylinders. A resistance usually consists of a length of wire made from a metallic alloy, such as German-silver, which, offering a considerable resistance to the flow of the electricity, causes it to expend part of its power in heat which goes to raise the temperature of the wire. The resistance, or "rheostat," must be duly proportioned to the work which it has to perform—*i.e.,* to the number of volts which it has to absorb and to the *quantity* of electricity which it must allow to pass. It will not vary according to the demand as a gas regulator will; but it may be procured in an adjustable form, so that the supply can be varied to a certain extent.

Of the electricity at the reduced pressure of forty-five or fifty volts you will require a *current* of from five to twenty ampères, according to the amount of light you will require. A fair average is fifteen ampères, at which you will get a light more than twice as brilliant as that afforded by the very best limelight jet. Regard this *current* as the *flow* or *stream* of gas required to produce the required light—not as its *capacity* as so many square feet. It is not practicable to measure the capacity of electricity, and so the flow or current is measured instead, and enumerated in ampères.

If you tell an electrician at the hall where you propose to use electricity for cinematograph work that you require a current of fifteen ampères, he will put up the necessary wires, or "leads," to supply you with that quantity. He will also tell you the voltage of the supply, and you must bring resistance accordingly. If he should inform you, in response to the question which you must not forget to ask, that the current is *alternating,* you may renounce all hope of getting a really satisfactory light; indeed, if you succeed in beating the best possible limelight you may be well satisfied. In the alternating arc two carbons of equal size are used, for a *quasi* crater forms on each. The light is distributed in all directions, so that you do not get any-thing like its full intensity; and it keeps up a constant humming noise all the time, though possibly that is not much objection where a cinematograph is concerned. Moreover, the light is very much inclined to vary con-siderably from minute to minute in point of brilliancy.

The last-mentioned objections are much reduced by the use of the newly introduced "eccentrical" carbons (invented by my father, T. C. Hepworth), in which the core of soft material is placed to one side in each carbon, having

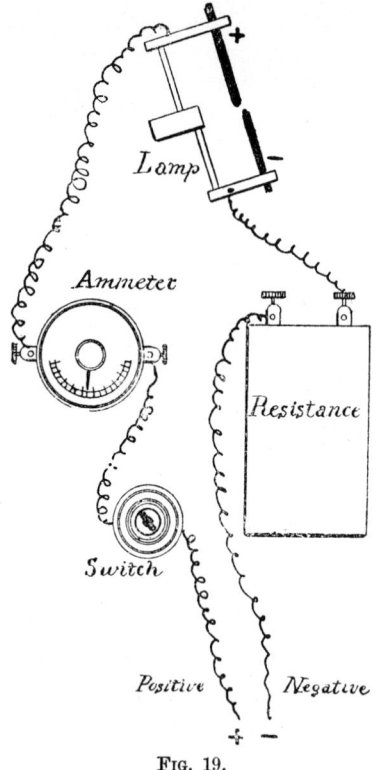

FIG. 19.

the result of causing the crater in each case to form towards that side.

In the case of the continuous current it is necessary to ascertain which of the leads is positive and which negative —which may be done by means of a "pole tester"—and to connect them to the lamp accordingly ; the former to the upper carbon holder, and the later to the lower. But between one wire and the lamp—it does not matter which —the resistance must be introduced. It is as if, after connecting the leads direct to the terminals of the lamp, one of the wires be broken and joined again by means of the resistance, so that the electricity is forced to pass through the latter on its way to or from the lamp. An ammeter (*i.e.*, an " ampère-meter," somewhat equivalent to a pressure gauge in limelight work) may also be included in a similar manner : that is to say, by breaking a wire and connecting the broken ends one to either terminal, so that the current is bound to pass through the instrument, if so desired.

The diagram (fig. 19) shows the arrangement of the wires and their connections. Great care must be exercised that no two wires are allowed to touch one another except where the covering or insulation is undisturbed, or the electricity may find a short cut across the place of contact, and, by operating the safety " cut-out " that the electrician will have inserted in the circuit, cut off the supply of current. The same remark applies to metallic portions of the lamp or resistance. A " short circuit " is sometimes made by a metallic tool, such as a screwdriver, slipping between two portions of a lamp, or other electrical instrument, between which there is electrical stress, and thereby providing the short cut of which the current is always ready to avail itself.

At the same time, you need have no fear of summary electrocution or of even painful " shocks." The shock from a hundred volt alternating circuit is perfectly bearable, though it is a little startling when you receive it unexpectedly. Where continuous current of the same voltage is concerned, the " shock " is scarcely noticeable. It is a different matter in the case of two hundred volts, but even then there is no actual danger. In this last case, to form part of the circuit yourself is certainly undesirable, for the sensation is by no means pleasant. Therefore avoid too close a familiarity : it will not breed contempt by any means—quite the reverse.

It has been said that the electric lamp is merely a

device for holding the two carbons in due relation to one another, and for feeding them together as they are consumed away. If you come to that, the limelight jet is merely a device for holding a piece of lime and directing upon it a stream of mixed gases. In both cases the description is a very meagre one in respect to the elaborated instruments that are alone capable of yielding the best results.

A good electric lamp for cinematograph work should have the following characteristics. Hand-feed lamps are alluded to, for, generally speaking, automatic regulators are liable to be considerably deranged by the vibration of the instrument. It is very little trouble to attend to a good hand-feed lamp, and it is certain in its action. All automatic devices are more or less uncertain, and are therefore not so desirable as the simpler instrument, which requires occasional attention, but is reliable. The lamp should be of solid construction, or the sympathetic vibration of the carbon holders will give unsteadiness to the projected light. The feed of the carbons should be either equal, and the carbon rods duly proportioned in diameter to burn equally, or the upper or positive carbon, being of the same size as its neighbour, should be fed towards it at double its rate. There should be an independent device for raising and lowering the luminous centre without interfering with the relative adjustment of the carbon points, in order to compensate for possible variations in their rate of burning. Lastly, the backward displacement of the upper carbon with respect to the lower should be adjustable; and it is certainly preferable that that adjustment may be made, if necessary, while the lamp is in action, for it is often desirable to alter it during the progress of a show. The feed of the carbons should be slow, so that their distance may always be adjusted to a nicety with ease—a matter of importance; and a "quick-strike" device, though not by any means a necessity, is a convenience, especially when, as sometimes in cinematography, the light has to be extinguished and relighted constantly.

CHAPTER IX.

COMBINATION OF LANTERN AND CINEMATOGRAPH.

A LIVING photograph show, from the showman's point of view, is a very difficult thing to manage properly. Every good entertainer likes his performance to go off smoothly and evenly, and without a hitch or pause, from end to end. But the longest animated photograph comes to an end in time, and that very abruptly; and then the question arises, what is to be done in the interval before a new one can be got ready?

There are several alternatives to choose between. You may continue to turn the handle of the machine after the film has run through, and half blind the audience with the flickering, brilliant white disc. That is the most inartistic alternative of all, and the one invariably patronised by the last-rate showman. By his works ye shall know him; and that flickering, palpitating disc denotes the born fool among lanternists. This alternative has several disadvantages. In the first place, it makes the audience cross, which is the worst thing that can happen to an entertainer. Secondly, it makes them forget the beauties of the last picture, no matter how good its quality was. Thirdly, it renders them unable to appreciate the beauties of the next, because their eyes are spoilt for the time being by the irritating glare.

Another plan is to cap the lens just before the picture comes to an end, and thus leave the hall in total darkness. It is a shade better than the other, but still it is very bad. It leaves the people with nothing to do, which is bad. It likewise gives them time to think, which they are much better without. Be your pictures the best that have ever been exhibited, there will be plenty of fault to find with them by people who have nothing better to do; and a certain gentleman, whose name it would be indecorous to mention, is even cleverer at finding mischievous employment for a large audience than for a single pair of hands. Possibly it pays him better.

A better plan is to have the lights of the hall turned up between each picture, but that invariably gives trouble. I have been to several halls where the tap on the gas main was right outside and had no by-pass. It does not require an active imagination to conjure up delightful visions of the lively "goings-on" which ensue when the female hall-keeper is put in charge of such a tap, with instructions to turn up the lights at the end of each picture (to which end she is to be notified with a bell), and to turn them down again in half a minute. Besides, the effect upon the audience is not good, even if you have electric lights and turn them on and off yourself, for the picture will not look so brilliant after the interval of light, and the "mischief still" objection may be still objected.

There are two more principal alternatives. One is to fasten all the films together in one length, and show them continuously without a break. You will require to be moderately rich in films, seeing that about sixty will be wanted to fill up an hour; and when the show is over, you will have the satisfaction of knowing that you have spoilt some excellent pictures by having too many of them.

Undoubtedly the best plan is to show one or two lantern slides between each animated photograph. The still picture is a great relief to the eyes and a thorough rest after the always more or less tiring living photograph. Its good qualities do not show up the imperfections of the animated picture when its turn comes, for the two things are so distinct and different that they are not mentally compared. And further, and most important of all, it gives the entertainer the opportunity of stringing his pictures together, to a certain extent; of making one follow after another with an attempt at natural sequence, which, if properly carried out, will do more to create a good impression in the minds of the audience than the most excellent photographs in the world shown higgledy-piggledy.

This being thus, it would only leave this little booklet unnecessarily incomplete were not consideration to be given to the various means of accomplishing the required result, and an attempt to see which is best, and at the same time most economical.

In one of the earliest cinematographs to be introduced—indeed, I think it was the very first to be shown in England—an attachment was fitted by which the light could be diverted by a mirror from the original instrument, and made to pass through a second, but precisely similar, optical arrangement, and thus to project upon the screen a title slide or other device while a new animated picture was being prepared. As the secondary lantern was only available for slides about an inch across—the size of the cinematograph pictures—its use was limited. In a later machine of a different make, a somewhat similar idea was carried out in this way. Above the cinematograph proper was reared a vertical lantern of the usual design, and of a size to accommodate pictures of the standard lantern size. When it was desired to exhibit a living photograph, the mirror of the vertical attachment was pulled out so that the light could pass freely through the cinematograph, but was diverted through an ordinary slide at the end of the film by merely replacing the reflector.

So much for the vertical attachment plan, which has much to recommend it. Here is another device which can be easily adapted with little trouble to most of the commercial cinematographs of the present day. Arrange the mechanical part of the instrument, together with its front lens, in such a manner that it can be swivelled out of the light (not intended in a slang sense) the moment the film has run through. Upon the same swivel let there be a board carrying a lantern objective of such a focal length that the image of the projected lantern slide will be of equivalent size to that of the animated photograph with the objective attached to the instrument.

I have used the arrangement hinted at—and, indeed, always use it—and find it quite as satisfactory as the more bulky and less economical biunial lantern that appears to be the most satisfactory alternative. For the benefit of others who may wish to construct the attachment for their own use, the diagram of the arrangement may be of use. The sketch (fig. 20) represents a plan view of the chief parts of the complete instrument. The actual cinematograph (meaning the mechanism and the short-focus projection lens), instead of being mounted direct upon the same baseboard as the lantern proper, is attached to a secondary base, B, of somewhat peculiar shape, and attached to the projecting lantern base by the bolt, G. Beside the cinematograph, and on the same level, but inclined to it at an angle of about 60°, is an upright supporting the ordinary lantern

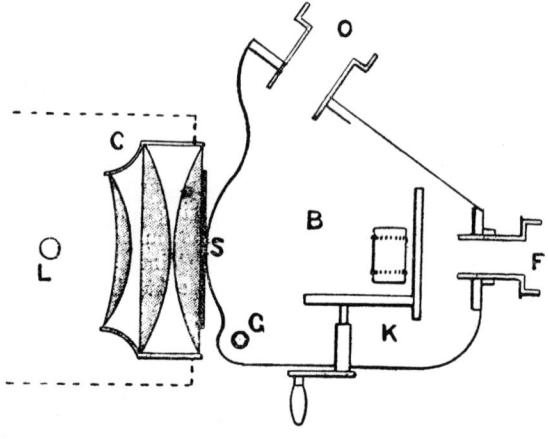

Fig. 20.

objective, O. The arrangement and measurement of the parts are such that when the base, B, is swung round upon the bolt, G, as centre, until the lantern objective is exactly opposite the condenser and slide, it will be at the right distance from them to yield a clear disc on the screen, if the light has been properly centred for the cinematograph. That is to say, the ordinary lantern objective, when in position, is at the same distance from the condenser as the cinematograph objective, when that is in position. A moment's reflection will show that this is the state of things required in order to obtain the **desired result.**

For when the lens, o, is in the position to project upon the screen the image of the slide, s, which is of standard size, it must be distant from it approximately its own focal length. Let us suppose that to be nine inches; in order to get a cinematograph picture of the same diameter upon the screen we must use a front lens of three-inch focus, for the diameter of a cinematograph slide is one-third that of an ordinary lantern slide. And with a front lens of this description, to obtain the best results it is necessary that it should be distant from the condenser—if of the diameter for standard lantern slides—by three times its focal length.

Now, in order to avoid the flickering white disc, as it is most desirable to do, it is almost necessary to attach to the end of the picture film a few inches of opaque blank film. If you have not such a thing at your disposal, paint out the last dozen photographs on the film with some opaque black varnish. It is far better to sacrifice a moment's animation (of the photograph) than to spoil its whole appearance by letting the clear disc be seen. Then, the moment you see this darkness come over the screen, cap the lens; stop turning the handle; slip the slide in the lantern—it should have been previously placed in one partition of a to-and-fro carrier; swing the other lens, also capped, into position, and remove the cap—and there you are. Then you will have plenty of time to change your film and plenty of light to do it by, but no heat to damage it.

To those who prefer the biunial lantern method—and it has many points in its favour—and who use the electric light, a simple and economical trick that I accidentally lighted upon a short time since may be of use. Let both electric lamps—which, by the way, *must* be of the hand-feed variety—be connected up through one resistance (*see* p. 70): that is to say, branch one of the "leads"—say, the positive—and attach one branch to the positive terminal of each lamp. Carry the negative wire to the resistance, and from that branch it to the two remaining terminals of the two lamps. You would naturally suppose that the current would divide and actuate both lamps to a less extent than if it had only one to look after; but it is not so. Bring the carbons of one lamp together, so that it lights up. It burns, of course, as if the other did not exist, for the electricity cannot pass across the still separated carbons. Now, "strike the arc" in the other lamp, and immediately the first one will go out, quietly, and without a protest. Light up No. 1, and No. 2 goes out again; and if the lamps be fitted with quick-striking devices, the change of light from one to the other will appear to be truly instantaneous. Moreover, the maximum current available may be consumed in each lamp, for they are never alight together even for an instant.

This method never fails, and it affords a very convenient plan for the operator who uses a biunial lantern for the exhibition of animated photographs and lantern slides alternately. Both lamps are always kept switched on while the entertainment lasts; indeed, switches are not necessary. Suppose the lamp to be burning in the lower lantern, to which the cinematograph is attached, and the film to be running through the instrument; then, the moment the film comes to an end—it is, of course, provided with the necessary blank piece at the extremity—the operator, who has his hand on the "striking" gear of the upper lamp, gives it the necessary movement, and instantly the upper lantern lights up and reveals the slide upon the screen, while the light in the lower one as instantly dies out.

CHAPTER X

PRECAUTIONS AGAINST DANGER.

THERE has been more than one terrible cinematograph scare. No need to advert to the horrible catastrophe that befell the unfortunates at a Parisian bazaar in the spring of the present year. The frightful calamity made far too deep an impression upon the whole civilised world for any to have forgotten it. It was caused by carelessness or crass ignorance. The cinematograph itself had little share in it, except, perhaps, that the highly inflammable films must have added considerably to the conflagration which followed the first outburst, and very likely turned what *might* have been—though it is not very probable—an extinguishable blaze into a conflagration that no available aid could quench.

As I have said, the terrible fire was in this case due to a cause entirely distinct from the cinematograph, which only stepped in afterwards, and added its quota to the general blaze. An ether saturator appears to have been the immediate cause, or, rather, the wicked carelessness with which it was used. It is reported that one operator refilled the saturator with the inflammable fluid while another struck a match for him to see by! But though the share which the cinematograph proper had in the catastrophe was but a secondary one, the general public have grown to bracket together cinematographs and danger so securely that it will take years of immunity to sever the connection.

It would be idle to deny the fact that there is a certain amount of danger connected with the cinematograph in careless or incompetent hands. Some there are, I know, who deny its existence altogether in this connection; but

it will generally be found, upon inquiry, that these persons
are interested in the sale of cinematographs or films or other
accessories. It is a most short-sighted policy, and is sure
to recoil on the heads of its originators sooner or later,
apart from the moral aspect of the question. And when
it is remembered that the inevitable relaxation of precautions, which follows upon the assurance from high places
that there is no danger, jeopardises hundreds of human
lives, the matter becomes something more than one of sharp
business practice.

But I do not wish to be an alarmist. It seems to me
to be both a wiser and better plan to call attention to the
sources of possible danger, so that they may be duly guarded,
than to altogether pooh-pooh their existence in spite of the
several accidents that have already been accredited to the
cinematograph. The danger, I believe, is little or nothing
where the just ordinary precautions are taken ; but that
it does exist to a certain extent, when such precautions are
altogether ignored, should be a matter of common knowledge. To deny it is just as idle as to chronicle the conviction that there is no risk connected with a paraffin
lamp, even when of the very cheap variety, partly filled
with low-flashing oil, and placed on the edge of a rickety
table in a room full of children; or to say that coal gas is
an absolutely dangerless commodity, when we have daily
evidence that directly a leak occurs, people *will* go and
look for it with a lighted candle. These are fairly parallel
cases. With paraffin and gas, accidents are occurring
every day, and will continue to occur, so long as people will
ignore the fact that certain conditions should be observed
in their use. There is no more danger connected with a
cinematograph than with a paraffin lamp or a gas bracket ;
but if it be used carelessly, and without any regard to the
conditions of safety, an accident is sure to follow sooner or
later, and when it does it is likely to be serious.

The sources of possible danger, other than those connected with any optical lantern, are these : the light rays
from the lantern are brought nearly to a focus by the
condenser upon the celluloid film bearing the picture. The
heat rays are condensed at the same time and from any
available source of light which is brilliant enough for

cinematograph projection; the condensed heat is powerful
enough to fire the film in about half a minute or even less.
Should the distance of the jet from the condenser have
become accidentally shifted, so that the heat rays are
actually focussed on the film, it will be fired almost instantaneously. In the majority of instruments the pressure
plates surrounding the picture point, whose duty it is to
retain the film flat at the focal distance from the objective,
are quite sufficient to extinguish the fire before it can
spread to the film spools; but if the film happen to be a
rather more than usually inflammable sample, the spurt
of flame may shoot up and thus ignite the free film above,
when there will be more trouble in extinguishing it. The
precautions against this accident are twofold. The film
may be held between metal pressure plates of sufficient
solidity to extinguish the flame by cooling should one be
started by the heat from the lamp, and an alum trough
should be used to lessen the chance of the film taking fire
from this cause. An " alum trough " is a cell composed
of two thick glass plates about an inch apart, and packed
at the three sides so as to make a water-tight box. It
is intended to be filled with a solution of alum in water,
and placed between the condenser and the film, so that the
rays from the former have to pass through the fluid before
reaching the latter. The effect is to shut out all the heat
rays and allow only those of light to pass through. In
practice it is found that pure water answers the purpose
quite as well, and if used in this manner will obviate all
chances of fire. This simple safety device should never
be omitted from the kit of the public entertainer with
animated photographs.

The other source of possible danger in connection with
cinematograph performances rests with the mass of very
inflammable matter represented by the heap of celluloid
which is usually allowed to accumulate in a basket or box,
or on the floor. It is all very well to say that nearly every
good machine is nowadays fitted with a winding spool to
receive the film as it leaves the instrument. Nine operators
out of ten will have nothing to do with such attachments.
These winding arrangements usually give a deal of trouble,
and they invariably cause delay in the exhibition of films,

for they rather more than double the routine that has to
be gone through between each picture. The attachment of
the end of the film to the receiving spool before commencing
to exhibit it is the most "finniky" job the operator has
to face, and the knowledge that an expectant audience
is impatiently waiting for him to finish is pretty certain
to make it take him longer than it otherwise would.

But all chance of danger in this connection can be
entirely circumvented without resorting to the somewhat
unsatisfactory plan of attempting to re-spool the film as it
leaves the apparatus. Let it be received in an ample bag
hanging direct from the film outlet of the instrument, or in
a box entirely closed in except the small opening necessary
for its reception.

So much for the alleged dangers of cinematography.
The situation may be summed up by saying that it is
unwise to blink the fact that, when the instrument is placed
in utterly incompetent hands, danger certainly does exist ;
but when ordinary precautions are taken, danger, humanly
speaking, is non-existent. By ordinary precautions I do
not mean the kind of thing which is sometimes insisted
upon by the London County Council : I am alluding to the
simple precautions that are naturally suggested by common
sense and a little practical knowledge of the circumstances
of the case. That august body appears to be without the
former commodity, and to have a rooted objection to calling
in the aid of the latter.

CHAPTER XI.

HINTS AND CAUTIONS: CARE OF CINEFILMS, ETC.

IN a previous chapter the great importance to the success of an entertainment of keeping an audience continuously amused was mentioned, and it was shown how the general merit of an entire show depends even more on a careful attention to the little details than on the excellence and number of the animated pictures presented; and this applies not merely to the professional entertainer, but quite as much to the amateur whose aspirations do not soar beyond the desire to amuse and interest a "few friends."

Remember, an audience is a thing of ideas. Keep it always and continuously entertained and interested; give it no time to notice and remember the many faults in your pictures; do not distract its attention by pauses and evident uncertainties; and lastly, but by no means leastly, never be tempted to surfeit it with *too many* animated photographs. It is said that a successful *chef* is careful to send to table only so much of his best dishes that the guests do not get quite as much as they would like. It is a good example to follow; and another leaf may be taken out of his cookery book by judiciously varying the nature of the successive courses so that one dish serves by contrast to accentuate the good points of the next. And it will be found that good lantern slides, artfully intermingled, will serve excellently as hors d'œuvres, appetisers, pick-me-ups, and post-prandial coffee.

The good effect of a living photograph show can be immensely enhanced by as far as possible stringing the pictures together into little sets or episodes. Group the pictures

together—wherein you will be greatly helped by the power to
introduce lantern slides, for of these there is always a greater
variety to choose from—so that one insensibly leads up
to another. This is not difficult if the pictures be studied
and care and thought devoted to them ; and, when well
done, the result justifies any amount of trouble. If a real
incident be not to hand on which to string the slides, let
an imaginary one be sought. It does not require very
great imaginative ability—the "argument" being there—
to construct a "plot" on which to hang it. The transitions
between the subjects being thus made easy for the audience,
it does not suffer from the weariness which is the inevitable result of watching a herd of heterogeneous pictures
—no matter how excellent—jumbled together without
rhyme or reason. By attention to these and like details
a good entertainer can make a series of very indifferent
photographs "go down" with his audience so successfully
that its individual constituents will go home in the full
belief that the pictures were thoroughly good, and the show
a most interesting one—all except a few knowing ones.
But let the pictures be the best that have ever been produced, and show them badly, with a "white disc" between
each, and a few pauses, and "stage waits," and dead
silences, and total darkness, and the audience will be tired
and discontented, and go home and swear the pictures were
the worst they had ever seen—except the few knowing
ones ; and serve you right, too !

One very excellent plan by which the trying pauses and
waits can be avoided is to join a number of films together
in one continuous length, and wind upon one big spool.
Between each picture there should be six or eight inches
of blank film, so that the audience does not get a foretaste
of the joy to come before there is time to stop turning the
handle or introduce a lantern slide.

It is not by any means a difficult matter to join celluloid
films, provided that one important detail be properly
attended to. That is, to so cut the film before joining it
that the picture or space in which the join occurs shall
be a whole picture's breadth ; otherwise, when the second
animated photograph comes to be projected on the screen,
it will be found to be displaced, with respect to the mask

of the instrument, and probably the photograph will appear cut in half and the halves transposed. To see the people in the picture bisected at the waist and their legs walking about on their heads may be a grotesque sight, but it is not pretty or desirable. When a piece of blank celluloid is joined between two subjects, the same care must be taken that the introduced piece be of the exact length to embrace a number—it does not matter how many—of *complete* pictures, no more and no less. This is ascertained by counting the number of holes between the end of one subject and the beginning of the next, reckoning from the division line in each case: if the number of holes—supposing the "four-hole" system to be in use—is four, or any multiple of four, the join has been made correctly; if not, another attempt must be made.

Two pieces of celluloid can be joined together by painting the surfaces to come in contact with a convenient solvent of celluloid, and then pressing them together until they adhere. A space of a quarter of an inch is ample to make a thoroughly strong joint in celluloid film, and after a little practice it will be found that a joint with half that amount of lap or even less can be made perfectly satisfactorily. It is necessary to remove the gelatine coating from the surface of one of the films to be joined for this distance from its edge, for a satisfactory junction can only be effected when celluloid comes in contact with celluloid.

Suppose that a film has been accidentally torn, and it is desired to join the broken edges. The tear, we will suppose, has occurred across the centre of one of the little photographs. Let us treat one end first. Cut away with a sharp penknife or a pair of scissors the remaining portion of that picture flush with its edge ; the film then comes to an end exactly at the end of one of the little photographs. Cut the torn end off the other portion of the film square in the same manner, but leave this time a "turning" of an eighth of an inch beyond the end of a complete picture. With a penknife scrape away the gelatine from the surface of this extra portion, so that the photograph ends, as in the former case, exactly at the end of one of the little pictures, but there is a small projecting tongue of clear celluloid beyond it.

With a small camel's-hair brush paint a thin layer of "solution" upon the tongue of clear celluloid and upon a corresponding portion of the *back* of the other piece of film to which it is to be joined. Without undue haste, and yet without wasting time, bring the two surfaces together; see that all holes which overlap are in exact correspondence; see also that there are four holes to each picture, including the one in which there is the join, and, being satisfied on these points, press the two surfaces as tightly together as you can, and in a few seconds they will be found to have adhered perfectly.

The mode of procedure when two films have to be joined together is just the same, except that care has to be taken that the *progression* of the picture is in the same direction in both cases. In taking an animated photograph, in the first place, the film is passed through the camera from above to below, and the image being, as in all cameras, inverted, the progression of a series photograph is always from head to feet, as it were—that is to say, if you hold up a strip of picture film in your hands so that the pictures are right way up, the earliest picture of the series will be at the top. It is never necessary, therefore, to follow out the progressive movements of the figures in a picture of this sort in order to see which is the beginning of the film. Draw the film through your hands so that all the figures pass feet foremost, and when you get to the end you will have reached the beginning—with apologies for the apparent paradox.

It will often be found when joining together two films of different design that the perforations will not in each case occupy exactly the same relative position with regard to the pictures. In joining them up you must seek a compromise and keep as nearly as possible to the required exactly four holes. As one subject changes to another on the screen, the second will of course be displaced slightly, either up or down; but that is quickly compensated by a slight alteration of the adjustable mask with which all "four-hole" machines are fitted. With the "one-hole" system of perforation this difficulty will not appear, because the position of the holes with regard to the pictures is always constant, and machines which belong to this class are not fitted, therefore, with the adjustable mask.

The "solution" or "film cement" with which the joints of films are effected is either a solution of celluloid and, possibly, one or two other substances, in a solvent such as acetone or amyl, acetate, or else the latter chemical used alone. Personally, I far prefer the acetate of amyl unalloyed rather than any of the gluey concoctions that are sometimes sold for this purpose, for I find it not only much cleaner to use and much quicker in drying, but, being perfectly mobile, there is little of the tendency for the surfaces to slide one over the other when pressure is applied, which gives trouble with the more slimy cement. Probably, however, it is quite a matter of taste.

With regard to the *progression* of the pictures, it is only necessary to place the film in the instrument in such a manner that the picture is upside down in the lantern (which, of course, is essential), and turn the handle so that it is drawn through from the top downwards, to ensure that the pictures shall be shown in their proper order. With some machines it is possible to work the mechanism backwards if desired; and with certain films, shown *à la* "Alice through the Looking Glass," the effect is extremely funny. It is a variation of the usual order of things which, if confined to once in an evening, is sure to raise a laugh.

When winding up the films after exhibition, see that they are placed upon the spool or other winding device feet upwards. If you pick up the middle portion from a heap of loose film—as you are sure to do, for the extremities have a simply wonderful knack of burying themselves—observe which way the feet of the people in the little pictures point, and then haul in the film in that direction, hand over hand, like so much rope, until you come to the end. That will be the end of the picture, in point of time, and that extremity must therefore be placed on the spool first. Attend to this, and the films will always be ready for use when required, and correctly wound.

The films should always be placed in the instrument coated side towards the light, as in the case of ordinary lantern slides. Some instrument makers, with badly designed machines, in which there are rubbing pads on this side, will tell you to turn the film the other way. Perhaps you had better do it when using one of these machines, or the gelatine will get terribly scratched; but if any lettering be visible on the picture, or it represent any well-known place, its topsy-turvydom will be very much apparent.

These longitudinal scratches on the film are a troublesome fault, giving the appearance of a heavy shower of rain to the projected picture, and it is one that was more or less inherent to all the early machines, in spite of the elaborate pads of soft velvet with which it was attempted to combat it. One ingenious theory, which may have some truth in it, supposes that the rubbing of the warm film against the pads the first time it passes through the instrument induces frictional electricity, which invests it with the power to pick up and attach to itself all specks of dust and grit with which it may afterwards come in contact. Certain it is that the film does in a most curious manner catch up an immense quantity of dust, despite the most carefully conceived precautions; and it is easy to see how in course of time the softest velvet would become choked with the grit, and form a veritable scraper to abrade the surface of the gelatine. So, in the latest machines, all rubbing pads and rollers and sprocket wheels and everything else with which the film ever comes in contact are hollowed, so that the surface of the film, both back and front, never touches any portion of the instrument except at the edges beyond the confines of the picture, where the perforations are.

CHAPTER XII.

CINEMATOGRAPHIC CAMERAS.

IT will naturally be supposed that the instrument by which the series photographs for the production of animated pictures are made resembles the projection instrument in many particulars. In many respects—indeed, in most—the two instruments are alike; so much so that in very many instances the one piece of mechanism serves indifferently for either purpose, though it is usual to make slight modifications—presently to be described—in order the more perfectly to fit it for the different conditions under which it is required to work.

The differences between a cinematograph for projection and one for the making of the series photographs are, optically, precisely those between an ordinary camera and a lantern, while, mechanically, the differences are far less marked. In a camera for the analysis of movement by photography—for that is what it comes to—the conditions are these : first, it is necessary to have the optical system, which consists merely of a suitable lens and a light-tight box in which to enclose the whole instrument—simply a camera; and, secondly, there must be the necessary mechanical device for moving the film to a fresh position after each photograph is taken, working in connection with a shutter which uncovers the lens at the moment that the film is stationary behind it.

In short, the instrument for taking these animated photographs is merely the simplest form of pocket camera fitted with a glorified roll holder. Imagine a pocket kodak built on a smaller scale and fitted with a lens capable of giving a fully exposed picture with a shorter exposure;

suppose the roll holder with which it is fitted to have a
capacity for, say, twelve hundred exposures, and to work so
rapidly by means of one handle that these can all be made
in the space of one minute,—and then you have a cinematograph camera. We talk about making "shots" with a
kodak, and as it is fitted for a dozen shots without
reloading, it may fairly be likened to a magazine rifle.
Then, if that be so, the cinematographic camera can only
be likened to a Nordenfeldt or Hotchkiss gun, for it will
rain a perfect shower of exposures in the time that the
simpler instrument will require for a single shot. Both
are deadly weapons in the hands of a good marksman, but
where one slays its thousands, the other slaughters its tens
of thousands. But here, you will probably say, are evidences
of the jawbone of an ass, and so to business.

One of the most important factors in good instantaneous
photography is always the shutter, and so it is only
natural to suppose that the shutter is an important detail
in the cinematographic camera. It is one of the chief
points of difference between a camera for taking the living
photographs and the projector with which they are ultimately reproduced. In the latter instrument the shutter
need not cut off the light absolutely in the intervals
between the little pictures; and in many cases it is found
preferable, as has already been explained, to riddle it
with holes, or otherwise make it partially permeable to
light, in order that the obscuration shall not be absolute.
But it is easy to see that for the making of the series
photographs no such compromise is permissable. The
shutter must not only be opaque, but it must fit so closely
to the walls of the cell in which it works that it is impossible for the light to creep round it by reflection, and thus
reach the sensitive surface at the wrong times, and cause
it to be fogged.

For this reason it is not usual to employ the cylindrical
shutter (*see* fig. 16, p. 53) for camera work; and where
it is used, it must be specially made to defeat the tendency
of the light to sneak in when it ought to be shut out. It
is more usual, because more convenient, to employ a
segment shutter (*see* fig. 15, p. 53), which is arranged
to revolve almost in contact with a fixed partition; or,

better still, to turn between two such partitions which are placed close to it on either side.

It is a common practice in cinematography to use a lens with the largest aperture that it is possible to obtain, and to make the shutter opening as small as possible, so that the exposure is always as short as is consistent with the lighting of the subject. Whether this is the best principle on which to work is a matter of question. It involves the employment of a shutter whose opening can be varied in extent with the brilliancy of the lighting and the character of the subject of each photograph; and the lens is used with the largest possible aperture, so that its defining power is always strained to the utmost—a fact which makes itself conspicuously evident whenever any portion of the picture is portrayed which happens to be behind its somewhat restricted focal range. On the other hand, if a smaller stop be used, all parts of the view, both near and distant, may be kept well in focus, while rapidly moving objects will not be caught with sufficient speed to prevent a slight blurring of their outlines. It is a question whether such objects are better portrayed with absolute crispness of detail when, as projected, they will appear to cross the sheet in a series of very rapid jerks, or whether it is better to have the stiller objects in perfect focus, and those that move rapidly to betray their movement by slight blurring of their vertical lines. Possibly the best solution is found in a compromise: the lens to be stopped down only so far as will ensure good definition over a reasonable range, while the shutter is not opened during the whole time the film is stationary, except under such conditions of lighting that sufficient exposure could only be ensured by that means.

As has been previously hinted, a large number of cinematograph projection machines are also available, with slight modification, for use as taking instruments. The modification consists, as a rule, of either of two devices: either the whole machine is detached from the optical portion of the projector, and enclosed in a light-tight case, the handle by which the instrument is actuated being re-attached from outside this case; or the instrument is originally made in such a manner that it is light tight, and it is merely necessary to attach two spool boxes, one above and one below, for the reception of the film respectively before and after exposure. In either case means must be provided by which the exposed film can be re-wound automatically on another spool after it has passed through the machine. Although such a device is often fitted to projection machines pure and simple, it is very rarely used, as it has proved more convenient to allow the film to drop out of the machine into a box or basket placed for its reception.

It must not be supposed that a cinematographic camera that is merely a converted projector is only a makeshift concern, and would naturally be inferior to an instrument specially made for the one purpose. It is not so by any means in most cases, though, doubtless, in some the adaptation is not so satisfactory as it ought to be. In the case of a well-known instrument, made on the " claw " principle, described on page 39—possibly the best machine that it is at the present time possible to procure—the machine is suitable alike for photography, contact printing of the positive from the original negative, and for projection. In each of its capacities it is unequalled by any instrument on the market, whether of the " triple purpose " variety or constructed specially for the one use alone. The mechanism is enclosed in a small box, and when required for photography it has two other little boxes attached in which the spools for the sensitive celluloid are placed and guarded from the action of extraneous light. This instrument is merely quoted here in order to refute the belief—common in some quarters—that a camera, to be satisfactory, should be designed and used for the one purpose only, and the same with the other two devices.

As may be supposed, the lens which is best suited for cinematographic projection is not the best for taking the series photographs in the first instance. Thanks, perhaps, to the great " boom " in animated photography, there is no lack of good lenses for either purpose. This branch of photography is bound to be, for the present at all events, so very expensive a matter that there would appear to be good excuse for economy wherever there is a suitable loophole. But it is no economy at all to use cheap and inefficient lenses : that were indeed a case of spoiling the ship for a ha'porth of tar.   When it is duly borne in mind to what a tremendous amount of magnification the little pictures made in the camera are intended to be subjected, it is surely unnecessary to point out that the definition of the original pictures must be beyond reproach. And then, when it is remembered under what peculiarly exacting conditions, as far as the lens is concerned, these photographs are taken, the necessity of using nothing but an excellent lens for their production will be apparent.

All the good opticians are making lenses for cine- matographic work, and a *good* optician does not risk his reputation by selling a lens that will not give satisfaction. Therefore go to a recognised maker, and pay a fair price, unless you are prepared to wade through many expensive experiments with numberless lenses, until you find one that suits you.   I am told that the " Stigmatic " lens, which has won such golden opinions wherever it has been fairly tried, has been adapted to cinematography with such success as one might expect from it when it is remembered that this glass will work at almost any aperture and still give perfect definition.   It is rumoured that for animated photograph work it can be made with an aperture of $f/2$, and under those circumstances cinematography in all weathers begins to loom large upon the horizon of immediate possibility.

CHAPTER XIII.

ON TAKING ANIMATED PHOTOGRAPHS.

IT has been thought by many that the future of cinematography will find its principal development in the hands of the amateurs, and there is certainly much precedent in support of the theory. But the taking of cinematograph photographs is a very expensive hobby, and not one to be lightly undertaken by him whose purse strings are not inordinately supple. The original cost of the apparatus, though considerably more than would buy an outfit of ordinary photography, is not sufficiently great perhaps to act as a serious bar to the pursuit, but the expense of the material to carry on the hobby is more than ninety-nine per cent. of amateurs could contemplate with equanimity.

The average price of a piece of negative film of standard size and ordinary length ranges from fifteen to twenty-five shillings, and the strip on which to print the positive costs as much again. The chief reason for its high price is the cost of the celluloid base on which the sensitive emulsion is spread ; and if in the future—as is more that probable—a cheaper, but equally efficient, material should be discovered, the expense of cinematography as a pastime might be very considerably reduced.

It is rather beyond the scope of this unpretending little manual to give directions in the by no means easy branch of photography which gives the title to this chapter. Nor is there much demand for such instruction; for, whatever may be the future of cinematography, it is certainly not at present an amateur's pursuit. The majority of persons interested in the living photographs, who have not taken up their production as a professional pursuit, have confined themselves, and wisely, I think, to the projection upon the screen of the comparatively excellent products of the cameras of professionals, and which are to be purchased in very great variety at a price which, considering all the circumstances, cannot be considered excessive.

But there are those who will wish, for the sake of completeness, if not for a more practical reason, to try their hands at cinematography; and even those who do not intend to dabble personally in the mysteries of the production of animate photographs may find a few brief particulars as to the *modus operandi* interesting if not profitable.

Every photographer knows the names of the few manu-facturers who hold the entire field for the production of rollable sensitive film. Naturally it was to these that the earlier experimenters turned for the sensitised material upon which to make their series negatives, and it is in the hands of these to-day that the whole trade in photographic film is to be found.

By the way, it is a rather unfortunate circumstance that both the material on which these series photographs are taken and also the finished photographs themselves, ready to be placed in the cinematograph, are vulgarly known as films. In ordinary photography we have, first, plates or films, then negatives, and lastly, prints or lantern slides. In cinematography we have films first, then negative-films, and lastly, films. It is sometimes very confusing.

The film supplied by the makers may be had either perforated to the standard Edison gauge or in plain strips of the required breadth, and up to about a hundred and twenty feet long in one piece. For commercial work it is strongly to be recommended that the film be bought unperforated, and that operation performed by the photo-grapher. For, to get the very best results in the matter of steadiness of picture, it is essential that the perforation of both negative and positive be exactly similar and exactly in correspondence with the sprocket wheels of camera, printing machine, and projector. But for the amateur who naturally does not wish to invest in the somewhat expensive piece of apparatus known as a perforator, the former plan will be more advantageous, and he will not object to pay a little extra for the perforated films.

The film, then, is placed in the upper spool holder of the camera in such a manner that its sensitive side will face the lens. The free end is then threaded through the instrument, and adjusted upon the sprocket wheels or other moving device in the prescribed manner, and finally attached to the receiving spool.

As to the focussing, that must be accomplished according to the exigencies of the particular instrument in use. In some you focus upon the film itself ; in others you focus for a test object at an approximately equal distance to those you are going to photograph beforehand on a piece of spare celluloid before you put the sensitive film in the camera ; and others you do not focus at all, for the camera is of the fixed focus variety.

Regarding exposure it is very difficult to say anything that shall be any guide to the worker. It has been well said that subjects which are suitably lighted and other-wise " possible " for the hand camerist may be safely attempted with a cinematographic camera. But the class of subjects that are fit food for the animated camera is naturally of quite a different kind.

The beginner may be recommended to practise turning the handle of his instrument regularly and rythmically at home before he attempts to expose a film in the field. As to the speed at which he should turn it, that depends to a certain extent on the character of the subject on which he is exposing, and to a great extent on the gearing of his instrument. It may be taken as a general average that the rate at which these animated photographs should be taken is about fifteen to twenty per second. For very rapidly moving objects the speed may be greater if smooth-ness of running of the projected picture be considered of superior importance to the length of film consumed for a given result; and for subjects in which the changes are very slow the speed may be less. It is hardly necessary to point out that the pictures should be projected at approximately the rate at which they were taken, although a slightly slower speed is often permissable.

With an instrument in which the handle is attached

directly, without any gearing, to, say, a "five-picture" sprocket wheel, the handle should be turned, generally speaking, at a not lower rate than three revolutions in a second. Set a metronome to beat seconds and "count three in a bar." It is an easy matter to deduce or count the gearing of your instrument, and you will be well advised to practise with it a little before taking it out for actual work.

There is nothing much that can be said with regard to the choice of subjects, but a hint or two as to the avoidance of some of the most glaring faults that are to be found in most of the commercial film pictures of the present day may be of advantage. In photographing crowds and street scenes and similar subjects—which always make more or less interesting pictures, having, at all events, the merit of being full of life and movement—precaution should be taken to prevent people passing just in front of the camera and blotting out the whole picture for a time with their huge and ill-defined forms. A hand-camera man chooses a time when such figures are not in the way : the cinematographer can do the same, but a hundred people may surge in front of his instrument before the exposure is finished. In the old wet-plate days the same might be said of ordinary photography, yet its practitioners somehow avoided the horrible results that are so frequent among the animated photographs. Surely if a living photograph, of all things, be worth taking at all it is worth taking a little extra trouble to free it from such a glaring fault as this. Recourse should be had only in the last extreme to placing the camera right above the people's heads, so that they cannot get in the way : the naturalness, and, therefore, the charm, of the photograph is to a great extent destroyed that way. Let the photographer take with him a few friends, who will stand near the camera, in front, but just beyond the angle embraced by the lens, and politely cause the passers-by to pass by somewhere but right in front of the instrument.

Again, the use of a wide-angle lens, nearly always reprehensible, is generally most abominable in connection with the production of a living photograph. The mere movement of the objects from place to place in the picture is sufficient to lend to it a heightened perspective effect,

7

which, in a single photograph, would be by no means so marked, and the exaggerated perspective of wide-angularism becomes horribly aggravated. For instance, what could be much more ridiculous than a representation of a boxing match, intended to inspire the spectators with excitement and dread, when the participants alternately dwindle to Lilliputian pigmies and swell into ungainly giants, as they dance around one another in the ring?

Little made-up comedies, carefully arranged and well acted (there's the rub!) make perhaps the most pleasing of all subjects for the living photographs, just as, when indifferently performed or evilly conceived, they are ineffectual or repulsive.

When advising a beginner in ordinary photography as to the choice and treatment of subjects, it is usual to suggest that he study the works of others and be guided thereby. But to the maker of living pictures let me say: Go, study the work of others, so that you may avoid their faults by all means, but do not copy any one. Think out some good subjects for yourself, and treat them in an original manner. There is a tremendously vast field before you, and up to the present it has scarcely been touched at the very edges. Above all, seek to make your pictures natural, for it is their reproduction of natural effects that nothing else can portray which is their charm.

CHAPTER XIV.

DEVELOPING, PRINTING, ETC.

THE real difficulties in the making of a series photo-graph for cinematographic projection are first en-countered in the darkroom. The amateur who purchases his film ready made and ready perforated experiences no particular difficulty in its manipulation in the field if he be tolerably familiar with the operations of ordinary photo-graphy. It is when he gets the exposed material home, and attempts to develop it and otherwise finish off the results of his previous labours, that the contrast to ordinary photographic procedure becomes more apparent and the manipulations more difficult. The development of a piece of flexible film, eighty feet long and rather less than an inch and a half broad, is an undertaking that may well make the average photographer shudder to contemplate. But like many others which appear so terribly formidable at first acquaintance, this is robbed of most of its terrors when you know how it is done; and, given the necessary implements, is not so very difficult after all.

Cinematograph films are usually manipulated in the darkroom by the aid of either one of two simple contriv-ances for reducing the unwieldy material to a form in which it is fairly amenable to the required treatment: either the long strip of film is wound upon a large drum or barrel, which is revolved with a portion of its periphery in a trough of developing solution; or it is wound upon a number of pegs set in a frame to keep the several convolu-tions from actual contact with one another, and can thus be completely submerged in the solution. Some workers advocate one method and some another. It is quite a

matter of taste. One or two other contrivances have been
suggested for successfully tackling and taming the wild
and unruly pellicle, but as I have never seen these in
actual use, or met any one who uses them, it is probable
that they are suggestions and nothing more.

To the thoughtful worker it will only be necessary to
hint at the character of the peculiar implements used in
the development and subsequent treatment of cinematograph
films, and he will easily be able to fill in the details, and
in all probability to make the several contrivances himself
with but little trouble. Fig. 21 represents the "drum"
developing device. It is such a simple affair that it needs

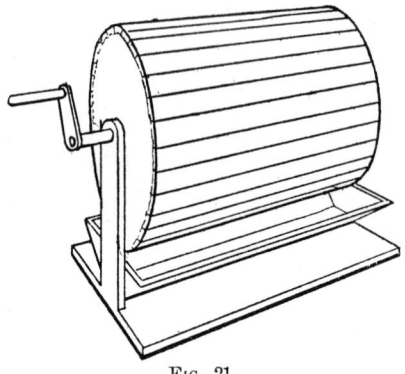

Fig. 21.

very little explanation beyond the sketch. As will be seen,
it consists simply of a wooden cylinder, closed at the ends,
and built up in segments after the manner of the roller
at the bottom of a theatrical drop-scene. Each end has
a central pivot by which the cylinder is supported on two
upright arms, so that its periphery just dips within a
shallow trough beneath; and one of the pivots is extended
to form an attachment for a handle by which the drum
is kept revolving in its trough during the progress of
development.

The method of using the implement is also pretty well
self-explanatory. Hold the roll of film as it is taken from
the camera in one hand, the fingers grasping the centre at

either end so that it can turn easily; draw off a short length, and attach the end (sensitive side upwards, of course), by means of a drawing pin, to the extreme edge of the drum; then turn the handle, guiding the film on so that each convolution takes up its position on the cylinder as near as may be to another, until all the film has been transferred from the little roll to the drum. Fasten the free end with another drawing pin, and proceed to develop.

A drum measuring fifteen inches in diameter—a convenient size—will, of course, comfortably accommodate four feet of film in each convolution, and, allowing an inch and a half for every layer of film, which is ample, a cylinder fifteen inches long will be large enough for a forty-foot film. A cylinder of twice that length will not be found to be too unwieldy, and it will accommodate a film that is as long as the majority produced. The trough may be as shallow as will sufficiently meet the case without running the least risk of the film rubbing against the sides, and the smaller it is the more economical it will be in the matter of developing.

With the constitution of the developing solution it is unnecessary to say anything to photographers, beyond a hint that it should not be one that is too easily oxydisable by exposure to the air, of which, as is obvious, it gets a good deal with this device. That objection does not apply to the alternative method to be presently described. Progress of development is chiefly judged by the red light shining upon the surface of the film; but towards the end of the operation it is advisable to detach one end of the film, and draw off a little, so that it may be viewed by transmitted light.

It is obvious that this cylinder need not be truly cylindrical, and may well consist of a number of laths, say, thirty inches long, screwed at the ends to two stout circular wooden hubs, fifteen inches in diameter, which any woodturner would supply for a few pence. Seeing that the cylinder cannot conveniently be made of one piece of wood, it is better that the necessary crevices between the segments should be wide than narrow, as in that way they are more easily cleaned.

The alternative implement for holding the film during

its progress through the darkroom is shown in the diagram
(fig. 22). It is a rectangular wooden cross having on the
face of each of its arms a row of perpendicular pegs an
inch and a half high, set a short and equal distance apart.
Here again the method of using needs but little explanation.   Attach one end of the film to one of the pegs nearest
to the point of intersection of the arms—the peg may well
be split for its reception.   Thence the film is carried around
the pegs similarly placed on the other arms, so that it forms
the sides of a small square box, as it were, the sensitive
side, of course, being away from the centre ; thence around
the four pegs just behind those already used, and so on until
the end of the film is reached and is attached in any

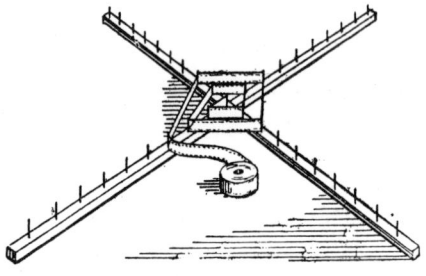

FIG. 22.

convenient manner to the last peg that it touches.   Thus the
film, when wound on this frame, forms a flat affair, which
can be totally submerged in the developing solution in a deep
dish of suitable size.   In fact, it can be treated very much
like a big glass plate ; and that is why, perhaps, this method
appeals rather more strongly to photographers than the
other.

     Development completed, the film is first thoroughly rinsed
to remove all traces of the reducer not only from the
surface of the film, but also, as far as possible, from the
many lurking places it will find around the pegs and
between the laths.   Then it is transferred bodily, together
with its supporting cylinder or cross frame, as the case may
be, to another trough or deep dish containing the hypo.

Next follows a very thorough washing, and finally a treatment with solution made up as follows :—

Glycerine	2 ounces.
Water	2 quarts.

Then the picture is finished, and should be allowed to dry spontaneously—still upon its support. After it has been resting for a few minutes, a plug of soft cotton wool attached to a piece of stick may be used to remove any drops of the glycerine solution that may have collected upon the surface of the film, and which might otherwise leave drying marks upon it.

As has been already pointed out, several cinematographs —notably those having the " claw " movement—are available for use as camera and printer as well as projector. When used for contact printing, two spools are attached in a light-tight box to the top of the instrument, one carrying the sensitive (positive) film, and the other the negative to be printed from. They are drawn together by the mechanism past the " window " where they receive the necessary exposure to light, and then the sensitive film is re-wound in the receiving box as in the case of the camera, while the negative falls out on to the floor or into a box placed to receive it. There may, of course, be variations of this, but it is the general scheme of the arrangement.

Generally speaking, the claims of those instruments, in which a sprocket wheel is the motive means, to contact printing capabilities should be regarded with suspicion. Where two films have to go together round one sprocket wheel there is a liability for one to creep upon the other, and the correct registration of the picture is disturbed. This undesirable result may have been guarded against in some cases, but it is as well to be forewarned. Printing machines specially made for the purpose have separate sprocket wheels for each film ; and in this case, of course, the movement is not intermittent.

The development and other operations to which the positive film must be subjected subsequent to exposure need not be entered into ; they will have been suggested by the remarks concerning negatives, to which they equally apply, except that such a developer must be used, and the process

only carried so far, that a clear, pleasant-coloured, and not
too dense picture is the result.   As a general thing, positive
films are much denser than they need be.   It is well to
guard against this fault, for there is no light to spare when
projecting a living photograph.   Let the positive films,
as the others, be well fixed, thoroughly washed, and do not
omit the treatment with glycerine solution after everything
else.

CHAPTER XV.

ALTERNATE PROJECTION WITH TWO LENSES.

WRITING in 1897 Mr. Hepworth states that animated photography is quite in its infancy. Indeed, it is only three or four years old, is still in a very incomplete stage of development, and some persons are inclined to think that it had been better for it, and possibly for all parties—except a few of its earlier guardians, who reaped substantial benefit from its early *début*—were it still in its nursery, awaiting a nearer approach to maturity. But it was destined to be an infant prodigy, and, in fulfilment of its natural destiny, was prematurely exhibited, proudly and nightly, to rapturously admiring crowds at all the music halls, etc., where it periodically brought down the houses in exultant admiration for its infantile precosity. Meanwhile, it trembled violently, was most erratic in its movements, winked and blinked and quivered, and otherwise exhibited evidences of its immaturity and incapacity. Let us hope it will not suffer the unhappy fate of so many infant prodigies, and, when the unwonted " boom " subsides, as it inevitably will, find itself entangled in a "slump" from which it has not the strength to extricate itself, for all its wriggling.

When animated photography does succeed in emerging from the depressed state which is likely to follow the present period of abnormal activity, it may be expected that it will have reached a far more advanced maturity. Already there are not wanting signs that the radical changes are being contemplated by which alone the present faults can be really eradicated. Some of the more earnest and thoughtful workers have retired altogether from the present struggle for supremacy, content to quietly perfect their

ideas until they shall have ready so accomplished an instrument that the world shall be taken by storm a second
time; others, who combine a keener business aptitude
with their science, and evidently think that a bird in the
hand is worth feeding and holding, though there are a
dozen fatter ones in the bush, are keeping up the supply of
the best machines they can turn out on the at present
recognised lines, while at the same time working out other
instruments on a new and improved system.

One new machine which is imminent, being built upon
an entirely fresh basis of, I think, a very promising description, is well worth mentioning before bringing to an end
this unpretending review of the cinematography of the
present day. If the view of persistence of vision, which
supposes that the image of any object persists upon the
retina with unimpaired brilliance for an eighth of a second
or thereabouts, were correct, living photographs which are
only " blinked" for a fraction of that time ought to appear
absolutely continuous; that is to say, there would be no
flicker at all. As that is very far from being the case, it
is natural to suppose that the persisting image occupies its
period of persistence in gradually fading away. That being
so, the only way to overcome the flicker which is still such
a bug-bear is by making the projection of the picture upon
the screen absolutely continuous. It is obvious that all
attempts to overcome the defect by shortening the interval
between the flashes can only result in minimising the
objectionable flicker, and never in its complete removal.
It is a "continuous illumination" machine which is pro-
mised us, and it seems to me that this is a larger step in
the right direction than has been made for a long time.

When you want to change from one lantern slide to
another with a single lantern, the best way to do it is
by covering the lens for a moment while you slide the
carrier through. You cannot make the change without
an interval of some kind, more or less unpleasant, except
by the use of a biunial lantern. So it is with the cinematograph. Several people have recognised that the way to
overcome flicker was to employ two projecting systems,
and actuate them alternately, but they did not see how
to do it.

Some have thought to gain the desired result by running two similar films side by side, each having its own set of lenses, with a rotating shutter covering them alternately, so that one picture is thrown on the screen to cover the flicker of the other. Besides the obvious one of requiring two films to serve the purpose of one, there are many disadvantages to this dodge which make it impracticable. In the machine under consideration the two optical systems are one over the other, as in an ordinary biunial lantern; and although there is separate mechanism for each, working alternately from one handle, the film passes through both.

The ingenious dodge by which the pictures are shown in their proper order by the two lanterns working alternately and yet the same " phase " of the picture is not projected twice, is this :—From an ordinary film negative, taken in the usual manner, a positive is printed by a special, but simple, machine, so that the " phases " are arranged in peculiar order. Along the side of this page is a diagram (fig. 23) of a piece of film showing the order in which the consecutive little photographs are printed. The first picture of the series is at the bottom, and it may be supposed to be in position for exhibition in the bottom lantern. No. 2 is fifteen spaces higher up, which is the correct distance to bring it into place in the upper lantern, the intermediate slack being absorbed by the sprocket wheels and rollers required to give the upper portion of the film the necessary intermittent motion. No. 3 picture is not next above No. 1, but is next door but one to it, the intermediate space being blank. No. 4 is a similar distance above No. 2, and so on, until by the time No. 15 is reached

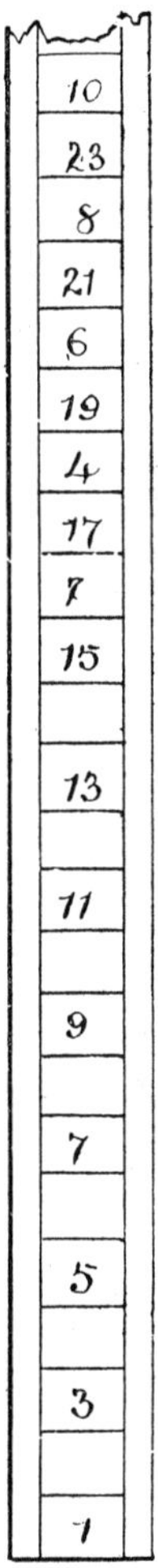

Fig. 23.

the later figures begin to occupy the spaces left between the earlier.

To follow out the history of such a film picture through the duplex instrument, we will suppose that the first two pictures are in position in the lower and upper lanterns respectively, and, the shutter being open in the lower lantern, picture No. 1 is on the screen. The shutter in this duplex instrument would naturally take the form of a single fan or segment alternately covering and uncovering each lantern, and so arranged that the process of covering one is exactly simultaneous with the opening of the other, so that there is no variation whatever of the quantity of light upon the screen. The shutter, then, rotates in front of the two lenses, and in the course of its revolution covers the lower lens and at the same time opens the upper. Picture No. 2 is thus thrown upon the screen, and the film in the lower lantern, under cover of the shutter, takes *two* steps forward and brings picture No. 3 into position. Another half revolution of the shutter and the upper lantern is again covered, giving the film therein the opportunity of moving two steps forward and bringing No. 4 between the lenses.

Thus a real step is made towards attacking the problem of the flicker from its very root. Already the uses of cinematography for scientific purposes are coming to be recognised; an appreciation of its possible services to education is likely to follow, and it is surely not too much to say that before long we shall see the instrument rid of most of its present imperfections and taking up its proper level as the lantern has done. That the cinematograph has contributed much to the gaiety of nations can hardly be denied, but that it will continue to do so to anything like the same extent for much longer is most improbable.

CHAPTER XVI.

NOTES ON CINEMATOGRAPHY IN 1900.

The First Cinematograph.

IN the introduction to the first edition, Mr. Cecil M. Hepworth does not give quite all the credit due to certain inventors who helped to initiate and perfect animated photography.

The shortest way to supply the omissions will be to tabulate in their chronological order the early inventions which bear upon the present practice of cinematography.

Although Patent Office and other records show that various efforts were made in and prior to 1888 to design a machine which should take, and exhibit by projection—or do either—a succession of photographs in such manner as to simulate motion, as far as the present system in use is concerned priority seems to rest with Mr. W. Friese-Greene. He it was who in 1888 devised a machine for taking and projecting which is essentially the prototype of all the varied patterns since brought out. That is to say, the machine in question took a succession of negatives upon a reel of celluloid film to which intermittent motion was given. The resulting positives were, in similar fashion, projected on to a screen. As far as the writer can find, Mr. Friese-Greene was the first to use celluloid as a material for obtaining serial projection transparencies; perhaps stimulated thereto by the publication in the above year (1888) of Carbutt's " Perfect Substitute for Glass," (flexible supports for photographic images).

Mr. Friese-Greene's machine was patented in June 1889,

when the specification was filed, and was shown at the Photographic Convention held at Chester in 1890.

August 15th, 1889.	Donnisthorpe & Crofts filed particulars of a rollable film cinematograph.
February 18th, 1900.	Brennan's apparatus.
March 8th, 1890.	Evans (intermittent film camera).
March 26th, 1890.	Varley (intermittent film camera).

The next notable steps were in

May 1891.	Edison's Kinetoscope announced.
April 1895.	Lumière's Cinematograph.
May 1895.	Birt Acre's Kinetic Lantern.
March 1896.	Paul's Theatrograph.
May 1896.	Maskelyne's Mutagraph.

All the above dates are those when specifications were filed at the British Patent Office, except in the case of Edison.

THE FILM : ITS SIZE AND MAKE.

Ever since the first edition of this work was published the battle of the gauges has been in full swing, with the result that the original size adopted by Edison for his kinetoscope is securing a monopoly.

In the first instance Mr. W. Friese-Greene attempted to work with a picture of the ordinary lantern slide dimensions —viz., $3\frac{1}{4} \times 3\frac{1}{4}$. The velograph employed a picture four times the area of the Edison film. The biograph film measures $2\frac{3}{4}$ inches in width ; the dimensions of its pictures being $2\frac{1}{2} \times 2$ inches. Inasmuch as the width of the last-named is twice that of the standard (Edison) film, which is $1\frac{3}{8}$ inches wide, each picture being $\frac{3}{4}$ inch high, it follows that to obtain the same result the speed of the biograph must be nearly thrice that of the smaller sized film. The biograph is consequently of very massive construction, and its mechanism, which is subject to greater strain and wear than the smaller machines, needs much attention ; it is also found desirable to drive it by means of an electric motor.

Admirable as the results are when shown, the expense of

such installation, the wear and tear of the large swiftly moving machinery, and film, the difficulty of transporting the machine, the greatly increased cost of film, etc., and above all the practical impossibility of showing the subjects obtained by all the other cinematographic cameras, have operated so that, while a few years ago there were in Europe several of these giant cinematographs in use, at the present moment, so far as the writer can discover, the sole survivor is the one which attracts such attention at the Palace Theatre.

Lilliputian Films.

From the foregoing it would seem as if the big film is as good as dead and buried. On the other hand an attempt is being made to popularise films which measure but half the width (or one quarter the area) of the standard films.

The advantages claimed for these are that of cheapness, and the extreme portability of the exposure-machine.

The best known of the aforesaid are the films supplied with the Biokam, and with the Birtac, respectively. The former is characterised by a method of perforation which is dissimilar to any other at present in use. The perforations instead of being on the margins of the film are in the very centre, between each picture. This system, while slightly reducing the height of the picture, adds considerably to its width. The accompanying diagram indicates the perforation by means of which the film is "clawed" down. (See pp. 38 and 43.)

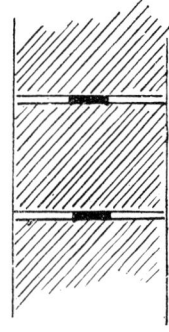

FIG. 24.

As regards the second of the two small films—that used with the Birtac—advantage has been taken of the ordinary Edison gauge four-hole film, which is cut longitudinally into two strips, and used so that two holes—instead of four, go to each exposure. The film is operated by a sprocket wheel, the teeth of which engage with the holes on one side only of the film. (See fig. 25.)

As regards the various brands of celluloid films at present

available little can be said except that, on account of their great liability to burn, all are the sources of ever-present anxiety. The Blair film and the Lumière one are well spoken of for general reliability, which is not surprising

when we remember that the manufacturers of both brands are also constantly engaged in making and printing negatives and positives for sale to the dealers. Hence, should there be anything amiss with the coating, or perforation, or otherwise, the operators, belonging to the respective firms instantly bring such defects to the notice of the manufacturing department. In other words what one makes for his own consumption is pretty sure to be wholesome food for the rest of the world.

Fig. 25.

In many instances the unsatisfactory action of projecting machines has been due less to their own imperfection than to the perforation of the film not accurately registering with the feeding devices ; to guard against which those who are well known for the steadiness and reliability of the finished films they sell, purchase the negative and the positive films unperforated, and perforate them with an accurately gauged " perforator," which exactly matches the mechanism of the taking and projecting machinery.

PROJECTION NOTES.

Many more or less ingenious devices have been brought forward to reduce " flicker " ; but its cause is not confined to any one particular portion of the machinery of projection. As already stated " flicker " depends upon the rapid alternation of extreme light, and extreme dark. As regards the cinematograph, " extreme " means *intensity* multiplied by *time*—i.e., 10,000-candle power shown for one-hundredth of a second would produce much the same effect from the " flicker " standpoint as 1000 shown for one-tenth second. The same may be said of the darkness. Hence one way of reducing contrast, which is the fundamental basis of flicker, is to so greatly shorten the period of total darkness that it is hardly perceptible to the eye. To the same end partial darkness has been adopted; and, going a step farther the shutter has been entirely dispensed with. This last expedient is in practice found to be unsatisfactory, amongst other defects the effect known as "rain" often ensuing. A good deal of the flicker sometimes met with is due to (1) The exhibition of films lacking in half-tone, and having glaring expanses of white sky, water, etc.; (2) the employment of an illuminant which is too brilliant. In early days the great cry in cinematograph circles was for "more light"; this notion has been handed down, so that most operators put on just as much power as they can get; this excess, when hard positives with clogged shadows are employed, may be a necessary evil; but in a good many cases where reasonably thin transparencies are in use, an over-powerful beam of light not only kills the images on the screen, but very much heightens the tendency of the machine to produce flicker. From the foregoing we may deduce that, in order to reduce flicker to a minimum, the movement of the film should be accomplished in as short a time as possible; the film should be free from staring, blank, high lights; and the illuminant should not be excessively powerful.

Undesirable Movement.

In too many instances the exhibition of animated photographs has been marred by motions not found in the original scenes portrayed. As regards these the cinematographist should learn to distinguish between the various, and in some measure unrelated, causes, so that he may be able to locate and, where possible, remove them. They are nearly all traceable to the following:—(1) Movement of the taking machine, produced by vibration set up by the mechanism, by a shaky stand, or by carelessness of operator in handling the camera; (2) "creeping," or other irregular registration of the positive and negative films during printing; (3) the feed of the projecting machine is faulty, or the film is improperly perforated; (4) the stand on which the projecting machine is supported lacks stability.

As regards the foregoing: (1) Cannot be cured except by retaking the subject, but may at times be somewhat ameliorated by having a dark margin to the sheet or screen ; (2) may be cured by reprinting; the devices utilised for printing are almost as numerous as the different projection machines—in some obstinate cases a change in the printing may be made which will cure the particular fault met with under this heading ; (3) if the machine is at fault all films will exhibit the defect; if only a few films show it, they may be considered to be the cause of the trouble. Let me now remind readers that they should not condemn any machine until after prolonged care has been given in testing it, and in securing the harmonious and effective working of all its parts. Remember, the mechanical feat which each machine has to perform is most remarkable. Thus in some cases—where the motion is to the period of rest as 1 to 8—the following operation has to be done to a nicety. Show an image for $\frac{1}{14}$ of a second and *within* $\frac{1}{100}$ of a second cover and uncover the image, and meanwhile replace one section of film by another, so that the latter is in accurate register and complete rest. That so much may be accomplished without any hitch presupposes that the particular machine has all its essential parts, not only properly designed, but made, fitted, lubricated, adjusted, and used. To the writer's personal knowledge one of the cleverest exhibitors of animated photographs quite recently bought one of the best designs of up-to-date projection machines, upon which the greatest care had been bestowed by the maker. None the less, although both man and machine were of the best, it took several days spread over as many weeks, before the machine could be got to work with the efficiency desired.

(4) In our days the principal offender is the stand. One which is both portable and rigid has to be found ; hence, when occasional displays by peripatetic operators are given, the animated photograph is apt to move a good deal more than is bargained for.

When movement of the pictures is caused by (1) or (4) its effect upon the spectator may be considerably neutralised by getting rid of all *marginal* motion. If, for instance, a picture be projected on to a screen having a white surface with a black margin (or frame) of about $1\frac{1}{2}$ or 2 feet, a slight movement due to either (1) or (4) will hardly be

noticeable.   If on the other hand there be a white surround
to the image on the screen the movement will become con-
spicuous by the dancing up and down of the margins ; this,
besides emphasising the imperfection, distracts attention
from the subject.

FILM FIRING.

One of the chief bogeys of cinematography is the ever-
present fear of conflagration. This is not without reason,
as the various flare-ups which have from time to time
happened bear witness to.   In many cases the alum trough
will remove all likelihood of the film catching fire by
means of the rays passing through the condenser.   But even
this is a source of danger, as if a sufficient proportion, say
20 per cent., of the solution should leak away, and evapor-
ate, during an exhibition sufficient heat might get through
to kindle the celluloid.   Besides air bubbles and other minor
troubles make the alum trough somewhat unpopular ; so
that, although probably every person who shows animated
pictures has the trough fitted to his machine, most of those
known to the writer rarely use it, but trust to their watch-
fulness, experience, and dexterity to see that, should the
film cease from moving forward the light is instantly shut
off.   While the film is moving at say 10–15 times per
second all fear of its catching may be dismissed, particularly
where the image thrown is fairly small, say up to 15–20
feet square.   That it is, however, possible to pass an
enormous amount of light—and therefore of heat—through
the film, providing a fairly rapid motion is kept up, is
evidenced by the Warwick Trading Co.'s exhibition at
Olympia when light enough to show a forty-feet picture
was passed through the small space of $1 \times \frac{5}{8}$ inches.   In
other words, the animated picture on the screen had an
area nearly a *quarter of a million* times greater than the
transparency.   The electric power called for by the arc
light was equal to 80 ampères—somewhere about 15,000
candle power !   Most authorities are agreed that the
main safeguard is to permit none but a properly trained
man to exhibit the cinematograph, if celluloid and a high-
power light are used.

Should a film unfortunately catch alight, in a good many

instances the pressure-plates and the general mechanism of the machine would either partially arrest the burning, or entirely stop it. The upper, or feeding, film would probably not burn at all, or but slowly. The lower film would be even less likely to catch if fed on to a winder or reel. But most operators prefer—or at any rate are accustomed—to run the films through into a metal or other receptacle.

It is under such circumstances that the most alarming outbreaks may happen; for should a spark from any source fall into a heap of loose coils of celluloid, and they catch fire, the whole would flare up with great rapidity, and although possibly there would be no great likelihood of the fire spreading, the audience would probably be panic-stricken, with the usual risk to limb and life.

For which reasons the operator should feed the film into some metal receptacle, a cylindrical corn-bin, or dust-bin will serve, and if the lid can have a kind of letter-box slit made in it through which the film is passed so much the better.

A fairly useful guide to safety is to be found in the Fire Insurance regulations, which have to be signed by those showing animated photographs in most of the halls throughout the country.

FIRE INSURANCE REGULATIONS.

re EXHIBITIONS OF ANIMATED PICTURES. *March* 1900.

1. The lantern must be constructed of metal or lined with metal and asbestos.
2. An alum or water trough must be used between the condenser and the film.
3. The apparatus must be fitted with a drop shutter available in case of emergency.
4. If the film does not wind upon a reel or spool immediately after passing through the machine a metal receptacle with a slot in the metal lid must be provided for receiving it.
5. If electric arc lights are used, the Installation must be in accordance with the usual Rules—*i.e.*, the choking coils and switch to be securely fixed on incombustible bases, preferably on a brick wall, and d.p. safety fuses to be fitted.
6. If oxy-hydrogen gas is used, storage must be in metal cylinders only.
7. The use of an ether saturator is not to be permitted under any circumstances.

POSITION.

Preferably on an open floor with a space of at least six feet all round railed off.   If in a compartment, the compartment to be lined with fire-resisting materials.

In any case no drapery or combustible hangings to be within two yards.

GENERAL.

Fire buckets to be kept filled, and a damp blanket to be provided and placed close at hand.

In the matter of my engagement at the .... Hall on ...., I agree to adhere strictly to the above regulations, and to hold myself responsible for any result arising out of the nonfulfilment of the same.

Signed,...

HINTS ON BUYING A PROJECTION MACHINE.

Before purchasing a machine consider how a supply of films is to be obtained.   At present films cannot be hired, as are lantern slides ; hence it often happens that the owner of a cinematograph finds but little use for it, as his subjects soon become stale and new ones are expensive, while old ones are by no means saleable.   Where it is decided to buy a machine it is well to bear in mind that there are a goodly few which will fail to satisfy audiences. None the less, as time goes on the makers of inefficient machines are gradually being squeezed out, and so to-day it is far less likely than three years ago that a purchaser will blunder on to an utterly useless pattern—unless, indeed, he goes in for a second-hand bargain, in which case *caveat emptor* !

It would be quite possible to name a few out of various makes which are well up to the average in their power to give satisfaction, but to do so would involve some injustice to others quite as well worthy of approval.   The best course to pursue is not to buy any machine unless one has seen it in action under similar conditions to those in which he wishes to employ it.

When a machine has been purchased and the purchaser has tried it and found it fail to act as was expected, let him be slow to blame it ; for with some machines a very slight, yet easily remedied, displacement of parts, or accidental want of minute adjustment or finish, will cause much trouble; then an unskilful disposition of lantern-elements, will impair the efficiency of the best machine. An imperfectly perforated "test" film will also make the action of a faultless machine seem imperfect. Apart from the foregoing points a purchaser should see to it that a machine works without much flicker or *noise*, and that it is fairly free from vibration. This latter defect generally depends upon the *balance* as well as the workmanship of a machine; by experimentally turning the handle at a fairly rapid rate one can approximately judge whether much vibration ensues.

Since the great rush of patterns a few years ago there has been nothing of any moment in novel designs. All the attention has been bestowed upon minor details, which, useful in themselves, by their numbers and insignificance baffle description. Perhaps one of the most prominent of these improvements is a device for adjusting the sprocket wheels which the Prestwich Manufacturing Company have fitted to their improved reversing cinematograph. The device in question very much facilitates the accurate centring of the picture upon the screen.

AMATEUR CINEMATOGRAPHY.

In the earlier days of animated photography doubts were freely expressed as to whether amateurs would ever be in a position to tackle this branch of photography. Since then the amateur has answered the question with an emphatic affirmative. Thus, amongst some of the most popular of the films received from the front at South Africa were those taken by an amateur. Another, who has obtained interesting subjects where the professional has not had a look in, is Mrs. Main, whose animated pictures of snow sports in Alpine regions are examples in point.

The cost of taking these fascinating pictures is no doubt a considerable obstacle to wide popularity, especially as the beginner is likely to waste much material while learning how it is done. This has, however, been to a large extent overcome by the placing upon the market of miniature machines, which, although in most respects doing their work with the efficiency of the full-size ones, bear but an insignificant proportion in cost of machine and material. Thus, a film which will run for about the regulation three-quarters of a minute may be purchased for 2*s.* 6*d.*

Perhaps the best use to which the remaining space at the writer's disposal can be put will be to recount his experiences with some of the small machines.

THE BIRTAC.

From first to last, in taking negatives with the Birtac, it worked without any hitch, except that the black strip of protective paper which, at the end of an exposure, should wind round the film, and shield it from the light, was at times apt to tear away at its junction with the celluloid this made it advisable to change the films, not in broad daylight, but with a cloth thrown over the camera. It is, however, only fair to say that others who use the camera have not found the above liability of the black paper to become detached.

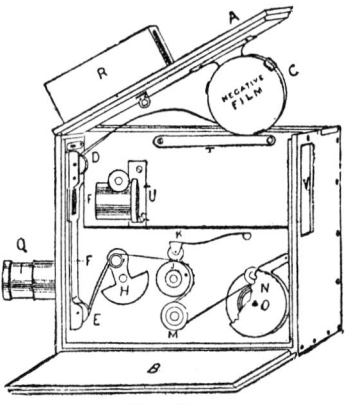

FIG. 26.

The charging of the Birtac, which, by reference to accompanying diagram, might appear intricate, may be effected *within about one minute.* The top, A, is unlocked, the side, B, let down, the film contained in a cardboard box, is placed in position at C. About twelve inches or more of the film are pulled out, the end passes over roller D is pushed down past lens at F, under roller E, over roller, H, between J and K, and round M into a spool at N. This may be done in broad daylight. Before shutting

up the machine, it is well to turn the handle once or twice
to ensure that the film is winding on spool, N, and that
the sprockets on J are properly engaging with perforations.
The camera is now closed and locked, and is so far ready
for use.

In making an initial exposure it is well to have all the
conditions as easy and simple as possible. The subject
should be one which keeps within the boundaries covered
by the lens, should move not too fast, and should be well
lit. The stand must be of rigid make, and should be so
planted that no shifting is likely to ensue ; or before the
end of the film is run through one may be taking nothing
but clouds, or, at any rate, quite miss the subject aimed at.
All things being favourable, the cap is removed from the
lens, and the handle which operates the mechanism steadily
turned at the rate of about three turns per second. This
may be considered as the standard rate, but with subjects
that move very slowly, and in a bad light, one may work
at less speed. On the other hand, in a bright light, with
objects passing quickly at right angles to the axis of the
lens, four turns per second may be given.

Caution in Exposure.

One point should be specially borne in mind when turning the handle, and that is to keep the motion as regular
as possible. Most individuals, in the course of every revolution, arrive at a kind of dead point, usually when the
handle is at the lowest part of its circuit. The result is
that every third picture receives considerably more exposure
than the average, consequently, as all are developed together, these exhibit the defect of over development, and
print out as under-exposed positives.

The accompanying illustration (fig. 27) will indicate the
fault referred to. A and C represent the normal exposure,
B over-exposure, due to irregular turning of the handle.
It is part of the first film exposed by the writer—using a
Birtac—and except for the defect in question resulted in
a perfectly satisfactory negative. It should be added that
slight irregularity of exposure and of resulting density in

the negatives may be disregarded as not materially detracting from the effect produced when a positive is shown on the screen.

Turning the handle at about three times per second, it takes nearly one minute to use up the film. But the tyro is advised to obtain his experience by making a series of short exposures, trying six subjects, to which ten seconds each may be given, under varying conditions of distance, diaphragm, lighting, and speed of exposure. If, when the whole spool has been used, the film is cut into yard lengths, the six exposures may be successively developed. By this expedient not only is a familiarity with the foregoing factors obtained, but the necessary practice in development is also acquired.

A

B

C

Fig. 27.

Developing the Film.

Having made a full-length exposure on a subject which is, presumably, fit to show on the screen, the first step to take is to cut a few inches off the end of the film in order to test whether the exposure has been under, over, or correct. This having been ascertained, by developing the trial strip, the developer is, if needful, modified accordingly.

This done, the film is wound upon a developing frame. A very good pattern is one formed of two rods at right angles, which are studded with pins in such a manner that, beginning in the centre, the film is wound round them so as to make a rectangular "spiral" (fig. 28). In doing this, see that the sensitised surface does not come next to the pins, and that the perforated edge is *not* at the bottom when the film is immersed in the dish. The latter should measure 12 by 10, and will require three pints of developer to submerge the film. It need hardly be said that most developers—except those containing liquid ammonia—may be employed. In the writer's case, a pyro-soda developer was used—1 drachm pyro to 50 oz. of water—and the other usual ingredients, including potassium bromide, in proportion.

The image should come up slowly (two or three minutes), and should finish in twelve to twenty minutes. While the film is in the developer, it is well to move it up and down from time to time, to ensure regularity of action by the reducer. The frame is next lifted by its handle, and, the

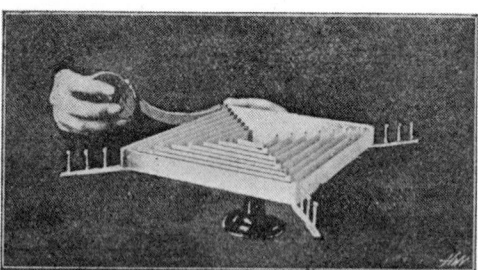

FIG. 28.

film being well rinsed, is placed in the fixing bath. It is then thoroughly washed, and soaked in a ten per cent. solution of glycerine for about five minutes. Finally it is dried. If care is taken to ease the film, the drying may be effected without removing the film from its frame, but there is always some risk of more or less serious damage, due to shrinkage. Wherefore, it is better to carefully unwind the film, and hang it up in an airy room free from dust. What is a still better expedient, is to wind the wet film round a wooden drum or cylinder. This results in the film drying flatter, and in better condition for travelling through the machine while printing. A very convenient and cheap

FIG. 29.

drum for this purpose may be made from a cheese box, which may be purchased for a few pence.

Instead of pyro-soda, metol-hydroquinone may be used, one advantage of the latter being that two or three exposures may be successively developed with one lot of solution.

The following may be used with advantage, subject to modification according to circumstances :—

Metol	.	.	.	.	.	50 gr.
Hydroquinone	.	.	.	.	.	50 gr.
Sulphite soda	.	.	.	.	.	$1\frac{1}{2}$ oz.
Carbonate soda	.	.	.	.	.	1 oz.
Pot. bromide	.	.	.	.	.	20 gr.
Water	.	.	.	.	.	20 oz.

Although a plain alum bath is sometimes necessary after fixing, it is best dispensed with, unless, through heat or other causes, frilling is feared.

The Birtac experimented with was used both carefully *and carelessly* without its mechanism getting out of order. The lens—by Ross—even at full aperture, gave a crisp image, and, when stopped down, using the smallest diaphragm but one (the values are not marked), objects within about 15 feet were fully exposed in a good light. The film sent out by the makers developed up with ease and regularity, and was commendably free from incidental defects. Altogether the writer was much pleased with the Birtac for its substantial make and its general reliability of action, while the facility of carrying a dozen films in one's pockets, and changing them between each exposure, is very useful, when, as sometimes happens, happy subjects come in crowds.

THE BIOKAM.

Another miniature cinematograph experimented with was the Biokam, which is certainly the most compact and ingenious, as well as the cheapest, little instrument on the market. Its appearance is indicated by the illustration, fig. 30. It measures but $9\frac{1}{2}$ inches by $5\frac{1}{2}$ inches by $3\frac{1}{4}$ inches,

FIG. 30.

weighs under $2\frac{1}{2}$ lb., and costs but six guineas—rather less than the average price of an ordinary hand camera. When it is remembered that the instrument is fitted with two Voigtlander lenses—one for taking, and the other for projecting—and that it can be used as an ordinary hand camera, or for time exposures; takes moving photographs, prints them, projects them, and can be used to enlarge them on to bromide paper, it is the source of much wonderment how it can possibly be put on the market at such a low figure. Without entering into minute particulars, it is here enough to say that the loading of the instrument is free from any noteworthy difficulty. A removable circular metal box, shown *in situ* in fig. 30, holds the film. The end of this is drawn out, passed between a spring-holder behind the lens, where the perforations engage with small strips of metal, and then are introduced through a slit into the "receiving chamber" at the rear.

In order to accomplish the above, the front portion of the instrument is made to turn on hinges; on closing the aforesaid and examining the back of the Biokam, a small peep-hole is found, which, being opened, enables one to see the subject to be taken focussed upon a portion of the film, the end of which is specially matted and left uncoated.

The shutters of the peep-holes which enable one to see through the "receiving chamber" must both, as soon as the picture is centred, be closed, or when the exposed film is passed into the receiver it would be fogged.

The Biokam is now ready to take the subject.

The above operations when once mastered are nearly as simple and short as, say, loading and focussing a daylight cartridge kodak. But inasmuch as considerable ingenuity has been lavished on the Biokam, and because several of the operations called for are unusual in ordinary photographic procedure, the beginner is strongly advised to *hurry slowly*, or disappointment may result, due less to the fault of the Biokam than to the ignorance or forgetfulness of the tyro. As might be expected from the size and weight of the instrument, although it is substantially and carefully made, it includes delicate parts which require attention, wherefore *il faut ne pas brutaliser la machine.* In fact, before putting the instrument to serious use, the amateur should test it by passing a spare film into the receiver, which latter is much the better for having been recently enlarged in size.

LA PETITE CINEMATOGRAPH.

This is another ingenious, compact and useful miniature cinematograph suited to the amateur or student. It possesses many of the features found in one or other of the two preceding machines.

Thus it is smaller than the Birtac, and rather more solidly made than the Biokam. The camera is charged by means of a film supplied in a light-tight box. This can be done in ordinary light. The free end of the film is passed over a stay, through the race, and out at the back into a receiving box. On the handle being turned, as the film is paid out, it is wound up on a reel in the receiving box.

FIG. 31.

Although on first reading the particulars sent out with the machine some people may not straight way understand how to put the film in its proper position, and how to prepare the machine for action, directly one has seen how the film is placed, and how the different adjustments are made, the procedure is ridiculously simple. Many people, to the writer's knowledge, have met with no difficulty in understanding and applying the printed directions. On the other hand not a few who have "tried" miniature cinematographs have never learnt the proper use of the instrument and its parts, and failing this necessary knowledge, have hastily and unfairly condemned this machine as inefficient.

The general appearance of La Petite may be judged of by fig. 31, which shows a front view with the front open. The machine measures but 8 × 4 × 3 inches excluding the receiving box, which is attached to the rear. In addition to exposing the film the machine prints, and also projects the positive. The film is clawed down in a similar way to the device used in the Biokam; but instead of a slit being between each picture, in which the claw or peg engages, there is a square hole. This allows the safe passage of film which is not quite correctly perforated; but the picture is consequently somewhat smaller. The film is wound into a small detachable receiving box. La Petite is made by Mr. W. C. Hughes, the well known optical specialist of Mortimer Street, Kingsland, N., and is splendid value for its cost, £5 10s.

Choice of Stand.

Of the various small cinematographs tried, all seem to lack a really good view-finder. The Birtac has one which is fairly effective, but it necessitates standing behind the camera, while the operating handle is towards the front. Sometimes when using the above on a tripod, this is not particularly inconvenient. But the best course to pursue, so that vibration and other movement should not ensue, is to place the instrument upon a solid support about waist high, and, bearing firmly on the cinematograph with the left hand, turn the handle with the right. In this position the only useful view-finder is one showing the picture from above. Some may be content to dispense with view-finders altogether, but they will find that it is well to keep a sharp eye on the cinematograph, which is not so easy if one has to be from time to time looking up to watch the subject.

Choice of Subjects.

As regards these, they may be classified into the known and the unknown.

In the latter case, however promising the beginning may be, long before the end all interesting incident may have given out. In which case, perhaps the best thing to do is to at once leave off turning, without moving the instrument, and resume turning when suitable incidents recur. Known subjects are those which have been noted and

timed, and which can be relied upon to repeat themselves
when being taken. Thus, every morning at 10.30 the
Grenadiers with band walk to St. James's Palace. They
can be timed passing a given spot, with a certain light upon
them, so that when the moment arrives the operator will
know when to begin in order that the interest is maintained
to the end of the film.

In a similar way rehearsed effects can be timed to a
nicety. With these, however, it is strongly advisable to
have an assistant, a kind of combination of stage manager,
drill sergeant, and time-keeper, who will keep the actors
up to their parts and see that they finish before all the
film is used up.

As to printing a positive film from the negative, and
exhibiting it, by either of the instruments described,
nothing can—or need—be here said, except that the writer
would counsel beginners to, in the first instance, let the
manufacturers of the machine used make the positives,
which they would do for three or four shillings.

"THE BIOKAM"
Showing detached parts of the machine.

Printed by Hazel . Watson, & Viney, Ld., London and Aylesbury.

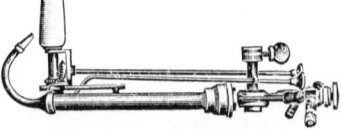

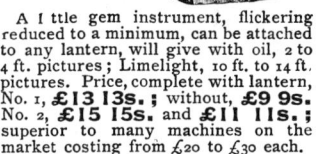